American Medical Association
Physicians dedicated to the health of America

Medical Practice Divorce
Successfully Managing a Medical Business Breakup

Joel M Blau, CFP

Steven M Harris, JD

Peter S Moskowitz, MD

Ronald J Paprocki, JD, CFP

Medical Practice Divorce
Successfully Managing a Medical Business Breakup

Internet address: www.ama-assn.org

Additional copies of this book may be ordered by calling 800 621-8335.
Mention product number OP208599.

ISBN 0-89970-990-7

BP37:0017-00:11/01

Contents

0479966707

About the Authors

Joel M Blau, CFP, is the President of MEDIQUS Asset Advisors, Inc, a national financial and investment advisory firm founded in 1996. Prior to forming the firm, Mr Blau was Vice President and Senior Financial Counselor for AMA Investment Advisers, LP, an affiliate of the American Medical Association.

Mr Blau has extensive experience in the analysis and design of financial plans and strategies for health care professionals. His areas of expertise include wealth preservation through estate tax planning, retirement, investment, and insurance planning.

A Certified Financial Planner, Mr Blau earned his bachelor's degree in business from Drake University, with a major in finance and a specialization in investments. His monthly financial articles appear in many state, county, and national medical specialty society publications as well as in several health care industry magazines.

Mr Blau is a well-respected public speaker and delivers financial seminars for the American Medical Association as well as other professional medical associations, hospitals, and clinics across the country. Recognized as one of the top financial planners for physicians by Medical Economics magazine, he has also been included in *Who's Who In Finance and Industry* and *Who's Who of Emerging Leaders of America.* He is a member of the Institute of Certified Financial Planners and holds various securities and insurance licenses.

Joel resides in the northern suburbs of Chicago with his wife, Susie, and two children, Jason and Jamie. He may be reached at 800 883-8555 or via email at blau@mediqus.com.

Health care attorney **Steven M Harris** leads a national practice assisting physicians and health care providers adapt to the increasing complicated legal and business environment of the health care industry. Specifically, he counsels physicians, physician organizations, and health care networks in mergers, acquisitions, dissolutions, and related contractual, transactional, and regulatory matters. He is particularly recognized for his representation of single and multispecialty physician groups.

Mr Harris is an often-sought speaker and author on health care issues that affect physicians. He is perhaps best known for his monthly column, *Contract Language,* which appears in *AMNews,* the weekly publication of the American Medical Association. Since 1997, Mr Harris has used his column to educate physicians and business health care professionals on confusing and sometimes dangerous provisions found in contracts.

Mr Harris has also served as legal counsel to the American Academy of Orthopaedic Surgeons in conjunction with its publication, *Contracting and Negotiating Managed Care Agreements* and contributed to *Before You Sign: Contract Basics for the Emergency Physician*, a publication of the American College of Emergency Physicians.

Steve lives in Deerfield, Illinois, with his wife, Jani, and sons, Ross, Marc, and Alec. He spends as much of his free time as possible fishing with his family. Steve may be reached at 312 280-0111 or via e-mail at sharris@hkgold.com.

Peter S Moskowitz, MD, is the founder and director of the Center for Professional and Personal Renewal in Palo Alto, California, serving the career and life planning needs of the medical profession nationwide. A skilled career/life coach, Dr Moskowitz is particularly interested in issues of life balance, stress management, and career transitions. His workshops and retreats, known for their pragmatic approach and ability to reenergize participants, are offered on a variety of topics related to physician renewal. His private coaching practice offers career/life coaching nationwide to individual physicians who are seeking career transition, retirement planning, and improved work-life balance. He is a consultant and lecturer to health care organizations on topics related to the changing health care environment. A practicing radiologist, Dr Moskowitz brings to his coaching work over 25 years of experience in both the academic and private sectors of US healthcare. He was previously Assistant Professor of Radiology and Pediatrics at Stanford University School of Medicine and currently serves as Assistant Clinical Professor of Radiology at the University of

California, San Francisco, and attending radiologist at the Good Samaritan Hospital in San Jose. Dr Moskowitz trained and was certified in professional and organizational coaching by The Hudson Institute of Santa Barbara.

Dr Moskowitz is married, has two children, and lives in Palo Alto, California. He can be reached at the Center for Professional and Personal Renewal (www.cpr.com) at 800 377-1096 or pmoskowitz@cppr.com.

Ronald J Paprocki, JD, CFP, is the Chief Executive Officer of MEDIQUS Asset Advisors, Inc, a national financial and investment advisory firm that specializes in assisting and advising physicians and health care professionals. Before co-founding MEDIQUS in 1996, Ron was the Vice President of AMA Investment Advisers, LP, an affiliate of the American Medical Association.

Mr Paprocki has been responsible for the analysis and design of individual financial situations for health care professionals, closely held business owners, and high level executives. His approach in assisting health care professionals has led to the development of The MEDIQUS Way,[SM] a planning method that utilizes a consistent and dependable process of analytical systems and investment strategies to help clients accomplish their objectives. Specifically, Mr Paprocki's areas of expertise include retirement, investment, and estate planning.

A Certified Financial Planner and Registered Securities Principal, Mr Paprocki earned his law degree from DePaul University College of Law and his bachelor's degree from Knox College. In addition, he holds other various securities, insurance, and professional licenses.

Ron is a regular contributor to *Medical Economics magazine,* which recently recognized MEDIQUS as one of the top financial planners for physicians. Mr Paprocki is also frequently quoted in the *Chicago Tribune* and has appeared on CNBC.

Ron makes his home in the western suburbs of Chicago with his wife and two children. He may be reached at 800 883-8555 or via e-mail at paprocki@mediqus.com.

Part I

Is It Time to Make a Change in Your Practice?

Where We Are

Certain signs or events—difficulty collecting bills, long-standing disagreements among your partners, the call schedule, or promising new medical techniques—have stimulated your desire for change. You may want to explore options and try a new practice setting. Maybe moving to another region of the country appeals to you. It may be that the original goals and aspirations that drew you and your colleagues together in a practice no longer animate that practice. If you are reading this book, you are probably preparing to make a major change. You may be leaning toward altering the way you practice your specialty or even leaving your practice entirely to start another career.

Where We Are Headed

To make a sound decision, you will need a great deal of information about how to plan a career change, what legal options and restrictions to consider, and how to assess your financial situation. You should read both chapters in this part, as they focus on the psychological aspects of decision-making and the legal agreements that can bind you to your current practice setting. Chapter 1 details the psychological preparation necessary to make such a change; Chapter 2 examines some of the legal and managerial reasons why physicians may chose to leave.

Psychological Preparation for Change

Peter S Moskowitz, MD

T he past twenty years brought profound changes to American medicine that continue to impact physicians professionally and personally like never before. As a direct result, the practice milieu, the emotional profile, and the coping strategies of physicians are undergoing change. Career dissatisfaction is growing and widespread. Increasing stress and burnout, substance abuse, medical disability claims, premature retirement, and alternative career planning by physicians are secondary signs of the growing crisis in American medicine.

For many physicians, the current climate will spur a decision to leave or relocate their medical practices. The focus of this chapter is to assess the factors that contribute to a decision to leave or relocate a medical practice. The ideas presented here emanate from experience with several hundred physicians who have attended physician renewal workshops or who have sought career and life coaching assistance.

Circumstances Leading to Practice Dissatisfaction

For decades the practice of medicine in the United States offered remarkable career stability. Steadily increasing demands for fee-for-service medicine and high levels of public esteem for physicians produced high levels of career satisfaction among physicians. Rigorous training was offset by an unwritten guarantee of high income relative to other professionals, broad public respect, and unprecedented practice autonomy. Physicians were the captains of the health care industry's ship. Health care income, as a percentage of the gross nation product, rose steadily. Few could foresee a potential need for change.

A complete discussion of the reasons for the change in this previously stable pattern is beyond the scope of this chapter. However, suffice it to say that the advent of managed care in the mid-1980s started a chain reaction that has permanently altered both the structure and function of the medical establishment. Over time, the work of providing health care services has evolved in specific ways that were unforseen both by physicians and by provider organizations.

The development and management of large multinational health care systems, mergers and consolidations, managed-care contracting, and increased competition among individual providers and systems of providers have permanently shifted much of the balance of control from providers to managers and from local sources to regional, national, and international systems. Managed care, including discounted fees for services, health maintenance organization/preferred provider organization (HMO/PPO) contracting, and capitated contracts, have driven physician reimbursement to significantly lower levels. Managed care has also resulted in longer service hours, shorter per-patient contact time, and limitations on the selection and availability of diagnostic tests, therapeutic services, and pharmaceutical products. Often, decision-making is done by others with significantly less professional training and expertise than physicians. Many physicians believe that the new rules degrade their ability to provide high-quality care.

As a result of this revolution in health care, the typical American physician has become more like an employee, with significantly less autonomy and control, less desirable working conditions, and faltering income. The result is stress. The new rules and demands of managed care have pushed thousands of physicians over the brink into feelings of depression, anxiety, powerlessness, and inability to cope. Unless significant efforts to improve self care and stress management are made, professional burnout often is the result.

Reliable figures for incidence of burnout in the medical profession are difficult to procure. A recent study conducted by the Sacramento-El Dorado Medical Society revealed a startling incidence of burnout among physicians in northern California.[1] In that study, 66% of physicians agreed that burnout posed a problem to patient care, 75% agreed that burnout posed a significant problem within their own practice group, and 40% admitted to being burned out themselves. The actual incidence of burnout is probably higher than these percentages suggest.

Factors other than stress and burnout often contribute to or are primary reasons for changing practices. These are discussed later in this chapter (see the section, "Primary Causes of Medical Practice Transition").

Understanding Common Physician Traits

Although it is hard to generalize about the personalities of all physicians, studies have revealed certain personality traits that are common among physicians.[2-4] Understanding these common traits may help to predict their responses to stress and their coping strategies.

Physicians tend to be driven and perfectionists. They are idealistic, hard working, dedicated, intellectual, and serious. Their ego satisfaction is often derived only from work and career, which explains physicians' relative lack of involvement in hobbies or interests outside of medicine. Through years of difficult training, they have learned self-sacrifice—to deny their needs while caring for others. Physicians often insulate themselves from their own emotions, and often they are isolated socially, with few intimate friends and few friendships outside of medicine. This often leaves them locked into their own thinking patterns with little emotional support or access to objective feedback from others.

Ironically, although most physicians are sensitive and caring of the needs of others, they do not always nurture or take particularly good care of themselves physically, emotionally, or spiritually. Fiercely independent, intellectual, and curious, they usually have an overdeveloped sense of responsibility, which fuels their tendency toward overwork and denial of their own needs. Despite their remarkable level of professional and personal success, physicians tend to be insecure and excessively self-critical.

Physicians' intelligence, independence, work ethic, integrity, and empathy serve them well as healers, yet their isolation from self and others often becomes a source of deep loneliness both within and outside their primary relationships. Because of their independence, pride, and perfectionism, most physicians are reluctant to admit neediness. They avoid asking for help until or unless they are in crisis. Because their comfort level gravitates toward stability, control, and predictable outcomes, they become uneasy and anxious when faced with change or loss of control.

Relying on this profile, it becomes easier to understand the current professional and personal crisis rampant among health care professionals. Unequipped to manage change, lacking plentiful social outlets for support and feedback, some members of the medical profession are anxious and fearful. They are reluctant to admit distress or to ask for professional help, considering it a sign of character weakness. Because they take poor care of themselves, physicians who make efforts to manage their own stress more effectively—by taking more time off or by working shorter days, for example—often also provoke feelings of guilt and shame. Concern about the success of their short- and long-term financial goals in the face of falling income contributes to their reluctance to reduce their workload. Paradoxically, some physicians may decide to work harder in a desperate attempt to stabilize income and to escape their increasing anxiety, only to find themselves emotionally, physically, and spiritually bankrupt.

Coping Strategies

The time-honored methods many physicians use to deal with stress and job or family problems are intellectualization, denial, avoidance, and work. Given an issue to resolve, physicians will typically turn first to their strengths: logic and reasoning. They will often seek solutions that require the least personal effort, and they may prefer to delegate responsibility to others. Still unsuccessful, some may choose to avoid confrontation with the hope that the problem will resolve itself spontaneously. Others may deny that there is a problem or try to resolve the problem through additional brainstorming about a solution. Blaming others for lack of success is common.

Such traditional coping strategies as asking for help (from friends, co-workers, or a professional), engaging in physical exercise, seeking emotional support (through psychotherapy, counseling, or peer groups), spiritual renewal (prayer, meditation, journal writing, or spiritual counseling), hobbies, increased rest, and relaxation are selected far less commonly by physicians.

Primary Causes of Medical Practice Transition

The primary causes of medical practice transition include stress and burnout, lack of life balance, physical illness and disability, behavioral disability, and skill-reward mismatch.

Stress and Burnout

Stress and burnout have become major occupational hazards for physicians. Although the problem has long been recognized, solutions are not always readily at hand.

The reasons provided by physicians for their own burnout are similar from one study to another.[5-7] In descending order of frequency, they include decreasing practice autonomy, loss of control in decision making, increasing work load, the encroachment of managed care, and declining income. By nature, most physicians are more comfortable in environments in which they can control workplace variables. To a large extent, managed care has removed them from this position of control. Not only is this a source of chronic stress, but also physicians are frequently not empowered to alter their circumstances with respect to managed care.

Another factor playing a role in burnout is the limited coping strategies of most physicians alluded to earlier in this chapter. Many physicians tend to deny their own stress and the feelings generated by the stress. Many feel guilty about their feelings of frustration or anger about their career, problems related to patient care, or their own emotional or physical limitations at work. For many, coping means working even harder in the hopes that in so doing, they will become too busy or too tired to have to deal with their own negative feelings.

What can physicians do? Those who suffer from stress might first focus on those issues causing the stress, and then strategize about only those stressors they can change. Some have found it helpful to make a list of the aspects of work that drain their energy and a list of those aspects that energize them. Finding ways to do less of the former and more of the latter is a simple formula to lessen work-related stress.

Lack of Life Balance

Almost without exception, the most important factor missing from the lives of most burned-out physicians is *balance*. Developing better life balance is the most potent insulator against physician burnout and can restore personal and professional resilience.

Unfortunately, life balance is rarely present in the lives of busy physicians. Many physicians do not have a clear vision of what life balance entails or, even if its value is apparent to them, how to acquire it. Many have lived their entire adult lives out of balance, believing it is the price they must pay to follow their calling to the practice of medicine.

Life balance means many things to many people. Following is a description of six domains of balance: physical balance, emotional balance, spiritual balance, relationship balance, community balance, and work balance.

- **Physical balance.** People with physical balance have good cardiovascular and neuromuscular conditioning. They are in good health and have abundant energy.

- **Emotional balance.** People with emotional balance are generally calm and centered. They are able to accept positive and negative input without excessive mood swings. They are aware of and are able to manage their feelings.

- **Spiritual balance.** People who have spiritual balance have a feeling of connectedness to self, to a community, and/or to a power beyond themselves. They feel a part of a greater whole and are hopeful rather than fearful.

- **Relationship balance.** People who have relationship balance are able to receive in their key relationships in proportion to what they give; they are comfortable sharing their own needs, wants, and reality with significant others.

- **Community balance.** People who have community balance have a relationship to a community of people who have similar interests. They give to that community of themselves in proportion to what they receive from others in that community. This satisfies the basic human need to feel a part of a community, and creates energy, gratitude, and selflessness.

- **Work balance.** People who have work balance are able to give of themselves at work enough to be valued, to succeed, to advance and to be challenged without losing their own sense of self or their own values.

Acquiring life balance first requires that people become aware of the absence of balance in their lives. During their training, denial of emotions and of physical and emotional needs becomes a survival tool for physicians. In medical school or even earlier, physicians-in-training are taught directly and indirectly to "work until the work is done," and to be sufficiently emotionally and physically tough that their own emotions or physical needs do not interfere with their duties to patients in times of emergency or crisis. As a result, physicians learn to perceive and solve problems around the needs of others, but not with regard to themselves. Although these skills serve physicians well in times of crisis, eventually many physicians shut down access to their own emotions so effectively that they are unable to be intimate or unguarded with themselves or with others. Not until the pain of their own isolation and loneliness becomes a problem, until their key relationships begin to fail, or until their physical health fails will some physicians reach out to seek help in improving the balance in their lives.

The equation to reach lifestyle balance will be unique to each person. A dynamic equation that will change over time, it will consistently lead to a greater sense of well being. To acquire better balance, physicians must learn to assess their needs in each domain on a daily basis. Self-awareness may come from a daily practice of listening to one's inner voice through prayer, meditation, journal writing, or quiet time alone. Over time, as balance and happiness develop, physicians often find that the value that they attach to this time alone increases. They learn that balance often results in their wanting what they already have—or, if not, it results in a decision to change those things that are under their control to get what they want.

Maintaining balance also requires that physicians assess their personal values and integrate those values into their daily lives. Balance requires integration of values, career, and private life to reinforce one's values and to spend as much time daily satisfying one's domain requirements simultaneously. Doing so may necessitate a minor or major career overhaul.

Balance in life is not obtained easily. It is especially hard for physicians whose education and training have consistently emphasized the value of doing and achieving over the value of just *being*. With this orientation, work may become the sole source of ego satisfaction and personal identity. As discussed earlier, work often becomes a coping tool for stress. Achieving balance is also difficult for physicians because they are often socially isolated, with few intimate friends. Without such friendships, physicians may have no consistent source of objective feedback relative to their values, choices, and behavior.

Pitfalls in achieving lifestyle balance include the following:

- The assumption that balance will be easy to obtain;
- A lack of personal commitment or a suitable support network, or both;
- A tendency toward perfectionism that may result in procrastination;
- Isolation that may result in being locked in one's own thinking patterns;
- Over-commitment that distracts the physician from giving adequate attention to his or her own needs;
- Preexisting addictions that support unhealthy lifestyle choices and that foster imbalance; and
- Financial overextension, poorly informed financial decisions, or an expensive lifestyle that is difficult to scale down.

Physical Illness and Disability

A physical ailment or disability commonly is the signal that immediately precedes a career or life transition for physicians. Physicians are not immune to diseases, and because they live and work under great stress, they are at great risk for disease. Although primarily an issue for mid- to late-career doctors, it obviously may occur at any age. Recent evidence indicates that disability claims to insurers by physicians are rising at an alarming rate.[8-10] This dramatic rise is related largely to emotional disabilities, including depression and anxiety disorders.

Systemic health issues forcing transition may include such acute events as coronary vascular disease, stroke, and trauma. Chronic illnesses may include malignancy, neurologic disorders, gastrointestinal disease, and arthritis.

Physical disability often necessitates modification of the workplace. This may include reduction in work hours, patient case load, night or weekend call duty, practice management responsibilities, or some combination of these. In the case of more severe physical disabilities, retraining in another clinical discipline or transitioning from primary care to practice management or administration may be appropriate. These issues and strategies can best be developed and implemented with the help of a professional career coach or counselor.

Behavioral Disability

As discussed previously, ample evidence exists that the changing medical environment is taking a toll on physicians' emotional stability. It is a tribute to the profession that so many doctors function so well under the conditions in which they work. A steadily increasing number of them, however, are ceasing to function effectively because of underlying or acquired mental disability, or both, which may include depression, anxiety disorders, bipolar illness, other psychiatric disorders, and chemical dependency. All may be exacerbated by stress. There is evidence that disability claims for emotional disorders are rising rapidly in the physician population; and monitoring agencies suggest that the rates of physician impairment from such disorders are rising, except for the rate of chemical dependency, which is stable.[11]

During recent years, interest has focused on the growing problem of behavioral disorders as exemplified by what is commonly termed the *disruptive physician.* Such physicians come to the attention of hospital medical staff committees and county medical societies because of their aggressive or hostile behavior toward other health care professionals or patients in the work place, or both. They repeatedly exhibit unpredictable, uncontrolled rage in conjunction with abusive language. The behavior pattern is pervasive despite verbal and written warnings and disciplinary threats. Disruptive physicians also experience a significantly higher rate of malpractice litigation.

Extensive evaluation of large numbers of such physicians has revealed a significant incidence of underlying axis I psychiatric illness and/or coexistent substance abuse and other addictions.[12] Frequently, affected physicians may have a history of severe childhood emotional trauma and significant adult career or life stress. Prognosis for improvement is good provided that appropriate professional intervention and treatment occur. Without intervention, recurrent job loss, reprimands, censures, and lawsuits may ensue. These setbacks frequently cause multiple career transitions unless or until the personal problems are addressed effectively.

Skill-Reward Mismatch

An often over-looked source of career dissatisfaction and transition is the mismatch between skills and rewards. *Skill-reward mismatch* refers to a physician's discovery, over time, that his or her particular medical skill set is not being adequately recognized or rewarded in the workplace. The problem may be that the particular skill set already exists or is over-represented in the local medical community. It may be that the physician's practice partners do not provide appropriate recognition through feedback or referrals; or financial remuneration may not reach regional or national norms. Regardless of the reason for the discrepancy, resentment is the byproduct of skill-reward mismatch. Resentment is a potent caustic that increases stress and erodes collegiality within a professional practice partnership.

What constitutes adequate reward is a highly individual equation that may change over time. Once recognized, mismatches must be analyzed from the perspective of whether or not adequate reward is a reasonable expectation, given the reality of the situation and the dynamics of the community. Although purely financial mismatches may be improved with dynamic marketing, nonfinancial mismatches are more difficult to rectify. The latter should raise a red flag suggesting the potential need for transition or relocation. Candid discussions with practice partners and referring physicians, while awkward, may provide objective feedback and improve communication between partners to resolve skill-reward mismatches. Many successful medical groups make time for such feedback at regular practice retreats.

Practice Alert: Understanding Mismatches

There are times when you feel overworked and underpaid. For many people, the difference between employers' expectations and what the employer is willing to pay is in fact their major mismatch. Other, less obvious mismatches may have greater effects on your career over a longer time span: Some practitioners discover that their personalities and skills are better suited to teaching or administration. Choice of specialty may prove troubling. Sometimes, it is hard to fit into the corporate culture or the tone and rhythm of a specific group practice. In fact, many highly qualified people who enjoy their work find that "fitting in" with a certain practice setting or employer may provoke the strongest feelings of mismatch. Taking personality-profile or skills-inventory tests may point out mismatches that do not relate simply to the size of your salary.

Mismatch of Expected and Actual Workloads Managed care has resulted in significant increases in the intensity of patient contacts per physician work unit in all clinical practices. This rise is particularly true in multispecialty clinics and HMO practice settings. For many physicians whose professional and personal life balance has been marginal, this change alone has been the factor to overwhelm them, leading to stress and burnout.

Work volume expectations when the physician first entered practice may have become significantly greater. At the same time, professional reimbursement has fallen by as much as 30% to 40% in may areas of the United States.[13] The reality is that physicians nearly everywhere are working harder for less. This may create a seemingly insoluble obstacle for many physicians who are financially trapped in an expensive lifestyle. Any efforts to reduce workload demands result in lower income, threatening the physician's lifestyle as well as long-term personal and family financial goals.

Financial issues have become among the most difficult obstacles preventing physicians from creating optimal work environments for themselves. However, falling income does not imply the need for practice relocation. Downsizing one's practice and lifestyle expectations can be important tools for coping instead. Values-based financial planning with a financial planning professional is also key to overcoming this daunting obstacle. *Values-based financial planning* means, in simple terms, that the physician and his or her spouse work together to discuss and prioritize what is most important to them as they think about their future. This process should consider what attitudes, assets, comforts, lifestyle, work plans, and financial responsibilities they desire or anticipate, and then designing a financial plan that assures they will have sufficient resources to meet those goals. It contrasts to the planning technique of aiming for a specific lump sum of money in order to reach "financial independence." (See Chapter 3, "Financial Planning to Ease Your Exit," for a detailed discussion of this topic.)

Other Contributing Factors

Additional factors contributing to medical practice transition include the changing workplace environment, personality conflicts within the practice, relationship conflicts outside of the practice, academic career cycle issues, changing skill sets, and retirement.

Changing Workplace Environment

Until the mid 1980s, the demands and expectations of medical practice were predictable, well-known, and relatively stable over time. This paradigm of stability was replaced in the 1990s by one of constant change. Drivers of the health care industry now include physician and nonphysician managers, mergers and acquisitions, globalization or regionalization of care, increased competition, total quality management techniques, and for-profit managed care. Implicit for physicians in all of these factors is loss of control, change, increased attention to the financial bottom line, and unpredictability. Without a strategy to accept and manage change, many physicians are doomed to increasing stress, fear, and resentment. As mentioned previously, "geographic solutions" to those issues—that is, relocating practice to an area where managed care has penetrated less deeply—will not provide a satisfactory long-term individual solution.

Personality Conflicts Within the Practice Setting

Traditionally, the American physician has been fiercely independent and self-reliant. Although these qualities and others have served physicians well, they also act as the seeds of interpersonal conflict within physician groups and organizations. Battles for control and leadership, gender issues, financial decisions, work habits, and professional "turf" issues are common sources of interpersonal conflict in physician organizations. In addition, financial and workload issues are becoming more common as reimbursement falls. Differences in patient- management decisions are less common sources of conflict.

The "Pack" Mentality A factor affecting interpersonal dynamics in physician groups is the pronounced incidence of what can be described as a "pack" mentality pattern of behavior. With this scenario, the most aggressive or hostile physician in the group will assume a leadership and decision-making role at the expense of the less vocal, more passive members. Attempts to create intimate dialogue between physicians in this setting often leads to derision or personal attack instead.

Physician groups function best when all members can openly speak their opinions without fear of derision, and in which all physicians have an equal voice. Problems are more likely to occur in groups in which there are inherent inequalities in decision making, voting, work time, patient load, income, or benefits.

Gender Issues   Gender issues also may become the source of interpersonal conflict. The proportion of female physicians in the work force is growing. Female physicians typically experience conflict around scheduling work time and time off to accommodate family needs and leaves for pregnancy. They are more likely than male physicians to seek part-time, flexible work hours; and the male medical community traditionally has been less supportive of such desires than many other professionals. The extent to which these issues persist today has not been studied systematically, although pregnancy leave-of-absence rules enacted in recent years in many states have had a positive impact in this area. As the proportion of female physicians and the growth of women physicians' organizations rapidly increase, concern regarding these issues should decrease over time.

Turf Battles   Professional turf battles have increased as sources of interpersonal conflict in medicine, largely among specialties. As reimbursement falls, the frequency and intensity of these conflicts increase as physicians try to sustain practice income through diversification of clinical procedures. Cross-training of procedural skills between two or more specialties is occurring in many residency programs. These conflicts are likely to increase significantly.

Work Habits   Work habits are becoming a more common source of interphysician conflict. As professional dissatisfaction grows, an increasing number of physicians are seeking novel solutions, such as part-time practice, flexible hours, sabbaticals, and no night call. Those fortunate to be able to sustain reduction in income by working less than full-time may experience the resentment of others less lucky. There is still a strong workaholic ethic within the profession that takes a dim view of part-time medical practice. Despite this attitude, the use of locum tenens physicians, part-time physician employees, and flex-time work schedules is becoming increasingly more common as physicians strive to find ways to reduce their clinical practice stress.

Relationship Conflicts Outside the Practice

Physicians' marriages fail at a significantly higher rate when compared to rates for the rest of the general population. In light of the stresses placed upon physicians' spouses by the long hours, fatigue, and emotional exhaustion, it is surprising that this rate of divorce is not even higher. Many physicians' marriages are sustained marriages of convenience for both spouses, although it is difficult to know how common this is.

Because of their work ethic, overdeveloped sense of responsibility and dedication, physicians typically place their clinical practice demands at the top of their list of time priorities. Therefore, given a choice between work and family, they will almost always choose work first. This choice commonly places an unusual degree of responsibility on the other spouse for child rearing, home maintenance, and planning the couple's social calendar. Over time, many spouses grow to resent the imbalance in the relationship. Left unattended, these resentments are often the first seeds of marital discontent leading to divorce.

Unmarried physicians face equally difficult challenges of maintaining a meaningful social, sexual, and recreational life outside the context of their busy medical practice. This requires unusual energy, creativity, and persistence.

Faced with the emotional, physical, and intellectual challenges of patient care, many physicians return home at the end of the day exhausted and either unable to sustain or uninterested in emotional intimacy with their family, spouse, or companion. Renewing the marriage must become a conscious task and a priority if it is to mature and flourish.

Divorce is less common than malpractice as a cause for practice relocation and transition. There is less stigma attached to divorce on the part of the physician, and child-rearing responsibilities usually motivate the divorced physician to remain in or near the community of the pre-divorce years.

Academic Career Cycle Issues

Physicians in academic practice may experience any and all of the traditional causes of professional practice transition mentioned thus far. In addition, the nature of academic practice introduces additional factors that may contribute to a physician's decision for career change. These factors may include problems with academic promotion/tenure, skill-reward mismatches relating to clinical care versus research, the politics of academia, and pressures relating to academic productivity and research funding.

Academic promotion and tenure are sources of career dissatisfaction that commonly result in job transition in academic medicine. Institutions in which basic research by faculty is highly valued create intense pressure on junior faculty to establish a research base, obtain outside sources of funding, and publish results to obtain promotion to tenure. Junior faculty commonly are also expected to teach, oversee the clinical care of patients, and demonstrate excellence in research as well. Few physicians are skilled at all three of these, and within this fact lie the seeds of dissatisfaction for many young academic physicians. Failure to obtain research funding, perceived lack of financial or political support within the department, or competition for declining numbers of tenured positions within academic departments leads many junior faculty to seek greener pastures at other academic institutions voluntarily. For others, failure to be promoted to tenure may obligate them to seek employment elsewhere.

Skill-reward mismatches occur in the academic sector of medicine also. Not uncommonly, faculty physicians—especially junior faculty—come to realize that their own skills and interests lie more in clinical medicine and direct patient care than in teaching and/or basic research. Occasionally the converse is true. Because it is natural to gravitate to those activities that showcase our job skills best, physicians experiencing such career conflict eventually must face the reality of their situation. They either fail to get promoted, or voluntarily find a position that rewards them financially and with academic promotion for the skills that they most want to use.

Changing Skill Sets

As physicians' careers evolve and mature, certain clinical or management skills often become stronger or more important, whereas other skills may become weaker or less important. Some may find that practice management is a better fit with their interests, skills, and temperament than is clinical practice. Others may lose clinical skills owing to changing patient demographics, resulting in less frequent use of certain procedures.

Physicians may lose interest in using special skills or in evaluating patients with certain specific problems that they perceive are more stressful or less challenging than is preferred. Older physicians may elect to stop performing certain high-risk interventions or surgical procedures. Other factors such as a desire to take less night or emergency call may play a role.

To the extent to which a physician's desires to stop providing certain services to patients are acceptable to the institution or medical group involved, there is no problem. However, when those desires are not acceptable to partners, groups, or institutions the dilemma may not be resolvable by negotiation and may result in the physician leaving the practice setting to find a more compatible practice environment.

Retirement

When physicians retire from the practice of medicine, they go through a natural transition process that is highly variable and individually defined. Full and complete retirement removes them from the rich professional environment that they have enjoyed and served in comfortably for many years. This transition to retirement living may not go smoothly, particularly if physicians have no well-developed interests outside of medicine, or if their financial picture or physical health is not stable. A life plan for retirement, derived with the help of a financial planner and a career professional, will go a long way toward easing the retirement transition. Aside from needing a plan that meets the financial needs of the physician and family, the retired physician needs a life plan that provides ample opportunities to find meaning, a sense of contribution, challenge, and fun. (A discussion of the details of such planning is provided in Chapter 3, "Financial Planning to Ease Your Exit.")

Practicing Part-Time   Increasing numbers of physicians are choosing full retirement earlier than they had planned or are electing to phase back from full- to part-time practice. In most instances, these decisions are reached in an effort to deal with practice stress and burnout. Practicing medicine part-time is always complex, often requiring extended negotiations with practice partners and medical groups. The latter often fear that part-time physicians will not be as committed to the business and administrative side of running a practice as full-time partners. There are issues to resolve regarding the allocation of patients, night call, salary, vacation and time off, and retirement benefits. These issues need to be considered seriously and responded to by the physician who desires part-time practice. Downsizing a medical practice obviously has a major impact on personal and family finances and long-term financial plans and commitments. These issues are best worked through with the assistance of a certified financial planner.

The Renewal Cycle as a Model to Understand Professional Transition

Many mid-career physicians were raised according to the paradigm that life proceeds on a linear path, and that their careers as physicians would be stable and secure. The changing times have proven these expectations to be unrealistic. To survive in times of constant change requires new ideas. The most important of these is the concept that life is *cyclical* rather than linear, bringing with it constant change and no guarantee of career stability.

The Cycle of Renewal, based upon the work of Frederic M Hudson, PhD, in his classic works on career renewal, *The Adult Years: Mastering the Art of Self-Renewal* and *LifeLaunch, A Passionate Guide to the Rest of Your Life* is presented in Figure 1.1.[14,15] The theory of the cycle of renewal is that during our journey through careers and relationships, we all pass through four common stages.

We begin in Phase 1, "Go for It." During this stage we have just completed training or education and we launch our career dream. We brim with excitement about our new career. We wake up looking forward to going to work. We are challenged and happy. We love our work. We also believe that it will go on forever this way. It is the American Dream. Unfortunately, for more than 90% of us, our excitement does not endure. Eventually, we all reach a plateau and Phase 1 comes to an end.

We quietly enter Phase 2, "Doldrums." In the doldrums we find ourselves with less energy. We gradually find ourselves becoming discontented with our work, sometimes just bored. We wake up not wanting to get out of bed. We no longer feel challenged. We hate it at work; we dislike everything and everyone associated with work.

We hang on because we harbor hope that somehow, some way, it is going to get better and be like it used to be. We are wrong; it will never again be like Phase 1. We feel angry and many of us end up spending years mired and miserable in the doldrums. Eventually, we realize that we must move on or stagnate forever. We decide what is not working and prepare to let go of it. This is very painful.

We evaluate our situation and find that we must take one of two paths to move on. The goal is to get ourselves back to an energized state. One option is to return to Phase 1 by cutting diagonally across the circle in what is called a *minitransition.* Alternatively, we can stay on the circumference of the circle and move down into Phase 3, "Cocooning."

In the minitransition, we elect to make some minor changes in our career, to reengineer our work, or learn an important new skill in our existing career. A minitransition typically takes up to six months and does not require learning a new career. It may not even require a new employer. With some form of new learning or reengineering we are able to reacquire enthusiasm for our work and find ourselves successfully back in Phase 1.

The more difficult and challenging exit from Phase 2 is to move into Phase 3, "Cocooning," and begin a major life transition. This involves a major letting-go and major risk taking. In the cocooning phase, we spend much time in self-reflection, investing in ourselves. We rediscover who we are, what is really important to us, and what our values and interests are. Generally, it is a quiet time. We may disengage from others and from commitments to do the work of introspection. We may start psychotherapy or read self-help books. We may learn how to meditate or keep a journal. We spend a lot of time alone, nurturing ourselves. We may quit our job or work less than full-time. Some of us may take a sabbatical or leave of absence. Others cocoon by taking one extra day off per week from work. As we cocoon, we naturally begin to discover new interests or remember some old, previously unexplored interests.

Figure 1.1: The Cycle of Renewal

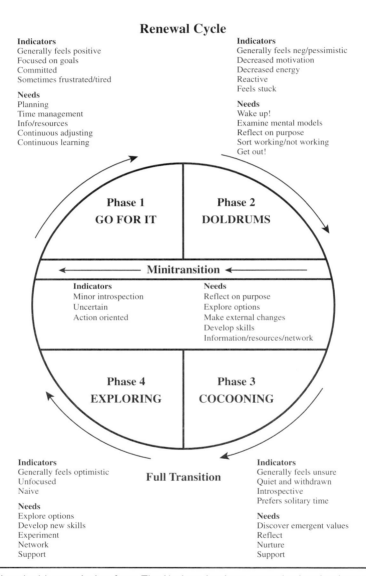

Renewal Cycle

Indicators
Generally feels positive
Focused on goals
Committed
Sometimes frustrated/tired

Needs
Planning
Time management
Info/resources
Continuous adjusting
Continuous learning

Indicators
Generally feels neg/pessimistic
Decreased motivation
Decreased energy
Reactive
Feels stuck

Needs
Wake up!
Examine mental models
Reflect on purpose
Sort working/not working
Get out!

Phase 1
GO FOR IT

Phase 2
DOLDRUMS

◄— Minitransition ◄—

Indicators
Minor introspection
Uncertain
Action oriented

Needs
Reflect on purpose
Explore options
Make external changes
Develop skills
Information/resources/network

Phase 4
EXPLORING

Phase 3
COCOONING

Full Transition

Indicators
Generally feels optimistic
Unfocused
Naive

Needs
Explore options
Develop new skills
Experiment
Network
Support

Indicators
Generally feels unsure
Quiet and withdrawn
Introspective
Prefers solitary time

Needs
Discover emergent values
Reflect
Nurture
Support

(Reprinted with permission from The Hudson Institute, www.hudsoninstitute.com.)

We begin to investigate those interests and as we do, we move into Phase 4, "Exploring." During this fourth phase, we begin to network with others who share our new interests. We find out more about our interests by taking new educational courses, or perhaps we retrain in a new field. We experiment with learning. As we do the exploratory work in Phase 4, we rediscover our passion and make a commitment to move forward with our new ideas and training. For some, it may mean practicing medicine in a new way; for others, it may mean a new fellowship; and for some it may mean simply a new hobby that inspires us. Regardless of the path we have taken, we are energized and passionate again about the next chapter in our life, which is about to begin. Although the movement from Phase 2 to Phase 4 has taken longer than a minitransition and proven to be more difficult and sometimes even painful, we again find ourselves ready to launch ourselves back into Phase 1, "Go for It."

What can be learned from this model? If we are stuck in the doldrums, how do we decide which path to take? The minitransition is popular with physicians. It is quicker, less costly, and less difficult than the alternative. It does not require the deeper inner work that physicians often find threatening. On the other hand, the minitransition is perfectly suitable for most people. One can do multiple minitransitions while trying to retain an otherwise satisfactory life setting. The minitransition has only one drawback: Each time you make one, the resulting new Phase 1 becomes progressively shorter. Sooner or later, many will have nowhere left to go and will have to make a major life transition.

In Summary

Major changes in the milieu of medical practice occurring in the past decade have had a major negative impact on the mood and attitude of practicing physicians. Managed care has led to a loss of autonomy and control of patient care, increased work pace, and falling reimbursement. Growing dissatisfaction, frustration, stress, and burnout have resulted in increasing physician disability claims, rising malpractice litigation, early retirement, transitions away from patient care, and medical practice divorces. The emotional profile of physicians often interferes with their ability to manage these stresses effectively. Doctors' training and work habits typically do not provide adequate coping skills or an appreciation of or ability to achieve life balance.

Other practice factors that may contribute to dissatisfaction, transitions, and practice divorce include physical and behavioral disabilities, medical malpractice stress, skill/reward mismatches, mismatches of expected and actual workloads, personality conflicts between physician associates, gender conflicts, turf battles, and work style conflicts. Factors external to the practice that may drive a desire for transition include failed marriages and other personal relationships; changing physician skills sets and interests; academic career cycle issues; and conventional retirement.

An understanding of modern career cycle theory permits physicians to escape outdated mental constructs and to acquire the skills needed to move away from feelings of victimization, fear, and helplessness in response to their career dissatisfaction.

References

1. Snyder M, Zvenko D. Physician Burnout Project: Sacramento-El Dorado Medical Society, 1997.

2. Gabbard G. The role of compulsiveness in the normal physician. *JAMA.* 1985;254:2926-2929.

3. Gabbard G, Menninger, R. The psychology of the physician. In: Gabbard G, Menninger R. *Medical Marriages.* Washington, DC: American Psychiatric Press; 1998:23-38.

4. Notman MT. Physician temperament, psychology, and stress. In: Goldman LS, Myers M, Dickstein LJ. *The Handbook of Physician Health.* Chicago, Ill: American Medical Association; 2000:39-51.

5. Edelwiich J, Brodsky A. Burn-out: stages of disillusionment. In: *The Helping Professions.* New York, NY: Human Sciences Press; 1980.

6. Lemkau J, Raferty J, Gordon R. Burnout and career-choice regret among family practice physicians in early practice. *Family Practice Research Journal.* September, 1994:213-222.

7. Musick JL. How close are you to burnout? *Family Practice Management.* April, 1997:31-46.

8. Kassirer JP. Doctor discontent. *New Engl J Med.* November 19, 1998;339(21):1543-1544.

9. Tye L. Disability claims by doctors soaring: physicians leave for big payments. *Boston Globe.* March 29, 1998:A1.

10. Pincus CR. Have doctors lost their work ethic? Physician's disability claims increase. *Med Econ.* 1995;72(4):24.

11. Meyers MF. Practicing medicine in Canada: what's happening to us and our families? *BC Medical Journal.* 1994;37:409-412.

12. Neff KE. Two hundred physicians referred for disruptive behavior: findings and implications for reducing errors in health care. Meeting proceedings at: Enhancing Patient Safety and Reducing Errors in Health Care. November 8-10, 1998; Rancho Mirage, Calif.

13. Moskowitz PS, Johnston M. Diagnostic radiology career satisfaction and needs assessment survey. *Diagnostic Imaging.* March, 2001.

14. Hudson FM. The Adult Years: *Mastering the Art of Self-Renewal.* San Francisco, Calif: Jossey Bass; 1990, revised 1999.

15. Hudson F, McLean P. *LifeLaunch, A Passionate Guide to the Rest of Your Life.* Santa Barbara, Calif: The Hudson Press; 1995, revised 2000.

Chapter 2

Why Physicians Leave a Practice: Examining Legal and Management Issues

Steven M Harris

There are, of course, many reasons why physicians choose to leave a medical practice. Some reasons would be considered justified universally: Proper planning cannot avoid the chance of becoming disabled, nor can it increase the likelihood of winning the lottery. These extraordinary events would not spark much debate if either caused a physician to leave a practice.

Proper planning can, however, reduce the probability that a physician will prematurely end his or her relationship with a group. It is essential to the long-term viability of any practice to invest in its most important asset—its personnel. Proper planning is cheap insurance that will serve to protect the essential relationships that will be developed throughout your medical career.

The Origin of Conflict

When problems within a practice do arise, they are typically caused by the inability of group practice members to resolve differences. And, most often, money is involved.

No matter how a particular conflict is described, the vast majority of disputes between partners originate with money.* Even when feuding partners agree that money is not an issue, upon closer examination, the distribution of money is often the main concern. (Rest assured, physicians do not have a corner on this market. Partners in all types of business bicker about money—whether in the form of compensation, equity, or both.)

By far the most common mistake made by physicians forming a group practice is the failure to discuss and agree upon sensitive issues, such as compensation, practice equity, and governance, at the onset of the relationship. There are few, if any, right or wrong answers to these critical questions. The lack of an exact solution or "textbook" approach to this process adds to the frustration level of physicians who attempt to tackle the task of designing these relationships.

Moreover, circumstances change over the years, and well-crafted legal relationships often require fine-tuning or sometimes a major overhaul. Anticipating these changes is often difficult, if not impossible. For example, how many standard employment agreements made just a few years ago contain information about compensation payable to physicians who treated patients subject to reimbursement in the form of capitative premiums? Remember, the types of arrangements discussed in this book allow for modification, so long as all parties to the agreement find the change acceptable.

Similarly, parties often operate outside of the strict legal interpretation of an agreement. Such conduct is typically acceptable—so long as all parties to the agreement continue to act in concert. Trouble often begins when partners turn to the agreement to break operational deadlocks or when one partner (or faction of partners) wishes to amend a particular provision within the agreement and the other side desires to maintain the status quo or modify the agreement differently.

Running a partnership on oral representations can lead to major misunderstandings. Setting forth—in writing—the parameters by which the practice will operate dramatically increases the likelihood that the relationship

---

* The text uses the word partner(s) throughout. Some physicians practice through professional corporations, others through limited liability companies. In these cases, the words *shareholders* or *members* are appropriate. The discussion is equally applicable to all forms of practice.

will survive difficult times. Written agreements may not contain all the answers, but the exercise of putting the documents together will force potential partners to examine whether they possess the common philosophy critical to a successful relationship. At a minimum, each partnership agreement should address compensation, value of practice equity, and governance.

Compensation

The methods by which providers of medical services are compensated within group practices fill volumes. Often, partners complain that a colleague is not working to his or her capacity, leading to friction within the group. When pressed whether the issue is properly framed as a compensation problem, the complaining partners, not surprisingly, initially answer along the lines of, "Bill is just not working hard anymore. He is taking too much time away from the practice."

Upon further review, however, a solution often can be found in an adjustment to compensation. Typically, the complaining partners doubt neither the professional competency nor the commitment to patient care of the problem partner. What they do object to is that the partner who is taking twice as much vacation or half as much call is compensated as they are.

The remedy is not overwhelmingly difficult. Initially, confirm that the subjective criteria for continued prosperity are still present: Do the partners respect and like each other? Do philosophies remain consistent? Is there a common vision for the practice? If most of the answers to these questions are affirmative, focus on the objective standards, starting with compensation. While compensation planning cannot remedy philosophical differences between partners, it can provide an antidote to disputes between parties who continue to trust each other and share a common commitment to patient care.

Time Commitment and Productivity

Adjusting compensation to reflect the time commitment and productivity a partner brings to the practice should be a clearly stated objective. Although revenue collected by the practice attributable to a particular provider may be the best indication of a partner's profitability and thus, his or her compensation, other factors should be considered.

A partner who provides administrative services to the practice, for example, does so to the detriment of personal productivity. Accordingly, the so-called "managing partner" should be compensated above and beyond what revenue he or she personally generates. Such compensation can be in the form of a percentage of practice revenue (eg, 1-5%) or a fixed dollar amount per year.*

Similarly, a partner responsible for attracting a disproportionate number of patients to the practice may require an associate physician to be responsible for the overflow. Compensating a partner with a percentage of the associate physician's productivity may provide an effective solution to credit the extraordinary effort of the patient-friendly partner.

As medical practices have increasing revenue from capitation, compensation formulas may well include factors for patient satisfaction, utilization of services (referrals for tests and specialists), attendance at committee meetings, and the efficiency of running the medical practice. If the medical group has a combination of fee-for-service revenue and capitation, the compensation agreement may have a certain percentage (eg, 60%) allocated to production and the other 40% to other factors.

Practice Overhead

Costs should also be analyzed according to the productivity of a partner. In the event a partner's productivity absorbs a greater amount of the practice overhead, such excess costs should reduce compensation.

Practices that require a detailed system for dealing with the allocation of overhead typically set forth three categories of expenses to be allocated

---

* Paying a managing partner 5% of gross collections, $50,000 per year on a $1,000,000 practice, may initially seem like a lot of money. On closer examination, note that if the partners (two in this example) each collected one-half of the practice's total receipts, the managing partner is really receiving only an additional $25,000 (or 2.5% of gross) for services rendered. The remaining $25,000 is compensation that the managing partner would have received through the compensation formula anyway. When viewed in this context, the amount paid to a managing partner who is performing effective service for the practice may be far less costly than the alternatives.

among the partners of a practice. These expense categories are usually fixed, variable, and personal expenses.

Fixed Expenses *Fixed expenses* are usually defined as costs incurred by the practice without regard to the use of the practice facility or productivity of the physicians. For example, rent or the principal and interest payments associated with the debt on a facility owned by the practice are typically categorized as fixed expenses. Fixed expenses are shared by the partners on a per-capita basis, assessing the particular expense as a fraction, the numerator of which is one and the denominator of which is the total number of partners in the practice. The fraction is then multiplied by the dollar cost of the expense to determine the allocation of the fixed expense per partner. For example, if monthly rent is $2,400, each of three partners would contribute $800, regardless of productivity or the time each used the practice facilities ($2,400 ÷ 3 = $800).

The costs associated with office personnel, including salaries and benefits, are sometimes categorized as fixed expenses, but typically treated as variable expenses. Practices that treat personnel (including associate physicians) as fixed expenses assume that each practice requires a receptionist, an insurance coordinator, or a technician regardless of the productivity of any individual partner.

Variable Expenses Perhaps the best method to allocate personnel expenses is on the basis of the revenue generated by each partner. Although far from exact, practices that treat personnel as *variable expenses* suggest that the more productive a partner is, the more resources are dedicated to the production of income for that partner. Accordingly, the more productive a partner, the more variable costs should be allocated against the income earned. Supplies used in the practice are another good example of an expense typically associated with production—and thus, carry a variable expense label.

Personal Expenses The third category, *personal expenses,* is seemingly straightforward but may often take some interesting twists. The more expenses properly categorized as personal to a particular partner, the closer the practice will come to fiscal accuracy. Truly personal expenses, such as entertainment or costs associated with continuing medical education beyond a fixed budget amount per partner, present no real debate about categorization. However, expenses such as professional liability insurance or health insurance are often treated as a fixed expense of the practice when, in reality, these costs are personal to the partner.

Compensation Formula

In the compensation formula illustrated in Table 2.1, premiums charged to the practice are determined per person. Even though an aggregate monthly health insurance bill charged to the practice may be $7,000, the partners will easily determine upon closer examination, the exact amount of the premium assessed against each employee, including partners.

By assessing the premium charged against each partner as a personal expense, with the remaining premiums allocated to the fixed or variable expense category—depending on the method used by the practice—each partner will more accurately pay for the expense attributable to his or her association with the group. This is especially relevant when partners age and family situations differ greatly. A partner who is single and 35 years old should not share equally in the premium cost associated with a partner who is 45 years old and married with children.

A similar analysis applies with respect to professional liability insurance premiums. The practice typically receives a yearly or semiannual bill for malpractice coverage. However, the invoice is simply an aggregate of the premiums associated with each physician, including partners. A partner who is rated because of a poor claims history should not receive the benefit of sharing equally with a partner who enjoys an exceptional track record. Similarly, a younger partner may be charged a smaller premium because the underwriting department of the group's insurance carrier does not treat that partner's practice as mature, thus resulting in a reduced premium within the same specialty practice.

Table 2.1: A Compensation Formula Including Variable and Personal Expenses

	Partner A	Partner B	Partner C	Total
Gross Monthly Collections	$15,000	$20,000	$25,000	$60,000
Fixed Expenses				
Monthly Rent	2,000	2,000	2,000	6,000
Monthly Principal and Interest Expense for Practice Expansion	1,000	1,000	1,000	3,000
Variable Expenses				
Salary and Benefits of Personnel	2,500*	3,333	4,167	10,000
Supplies	250	333	417	1,000
Professional Liability Monthly Premiums (associate physicians = 3 x 500)	375	500	625	1,500
Personal Expenses				
Monthly Health Insurance Premium (Personal)	300	420	510	1,230
Auto lease	450	400	650	1,500
Total Monthly Expenses	<6,875>	<7,986>	<9,369>	<24,230>
Partner Monthly Compensation Before Taxes	$8,125	$12,014	$15,631	$35,770

* ($15,000 ÷ $60,000) × $10,000 = $2,500

Practice Equity

Practices often attempt to match the equity of a practice to a partner's compensation. However, the concepts of equity and compensation are remarkably different and should not be confused.

There is no rule or principle that mandates that compensation paid to a partner should be proportionate to his or her equity stake in the practice. Refer again to Table 2.1. Partners A, B, and C may each own an equal equity percentage in the practice, yet their compensation is based on productivity. However, their equity may entitle them by agreement to an equal distribution of profits associated with employed physicians of the practice, an example of which is shown in Table 2.2.

Table 2.2: A Compensation Formula Dividing Profits from Associate Physicians Equally

	Partner A	Partner B	Partner C	Total
Partner Monthly Compensation before Taxes (from Table 2.1)	$8,125	$12,014	$15,631	$35,770
Associate Physician Monthly Profit*	4,000	4,000	4,000	12,000
Total Partner Monthly Compensation	$12,125	$16,014	$19,631	$47,770

When a practice elects to share the profits associated with employed physicians equally among all partners as set forth above, the expenses associated with the production of income are typically shared equally. The table depicts expenses associated with employed physicians allocated based upon partner productivity. Although certainly not governed by a specific rule, practices usually elect to treat revenues and expenses associated with a particular item consistently.

Group practices today are selling, merging, consolidating, and affiliating in record numbers. Whether a group practice should entertain such a business combination is often the focus of intense internal debate. In large part, although physicians outwardly discuss what is best for the practice, what goes on in each physician's mind centers on what the proposed transaction will personally mean to *him* or *her.* Partners should focus their decision making on the benefit of the transaction to the *practice,* placing their own personal financial stakes in the outcome a distant second. While perhaps an idealistic goal, creating equal financial incentives among partners facing a career-altering event will more freely foster constructive dialogue.

Multispecialty Practices

The disparate compensation issue is most dramatically found in multi-specialty practices. Perhaps, specialists are compensated using a formula that takes into account their ability to generate more professional fees than are their primary-care partners. As is often the case however, the primary-care physicians are most responsible for the number of patients seen by the specialists, thus enabling the specialists to generate more fees for the practice—and earn greater compensation. The relationship is truly symbiotic, in that each type of partner (primary care and specialist) contributes equally to the value of the practice as a whole.

The practice may decide to adopt a hybrid approach in which the proportion of the entity owned by each partner is of equal value and the outstanding accounts receivable (which are typically not included as part of the sale) are paid to each partner in proportion to productivity relative to all other partners. Adopting a business model in which all partners gain or lose equally in connection with a proposed business combination will lessen the likelihood that a partner or faction of partners will endorse such a transaction mainly for personal gain.

Governance

Like the relationship between compensation and value of practice equity, no direct relationship need exist between money and governing power. The amount of compensation a partner is entitled to, pursuant to an agreed-upon formula, need not correspond to the weight his or her vote carries on partnership matters. Many group practices subscribe to the "one partner-one vote" theory, regardless of the earning potential of a particular physician. Structuring proper governing agreements within a partnership relationship may lead to the success or failure of the practice.

As a practice grows in number of physicians, a centralized management structure is advisable. Practices that employ ten or more physicians should consider a board of directors or similar management committee of three to represent the group. Even in these situations, major decisions outside of the ordinary course of business should be ratified by at least a simple majority of the partners. Some decisions are so extraordinary that the approval of the governing board and the affirmative vote of a super-majority of the partners is appropriate. Examples of extraordinary events for which group practices should consider requiring a supermajority vote may be a merger, sale, or dissolution of the practice, and the termination of a physician without a specific defined cause.

Group practices that employ fewer than ten physicians may adopt many of the governing structures of larger groups. In those cases, however, there may be no need for an independent board of directors or executive committee to govern the practice. In every case, the more important the issue, the more partners should participate in the decision-making process.

Partners (physicians with equity positions) should meet annually to discuss the partnership agreement, particularly the compensation agreement. As the medical environment changes in which the medical group is competing, the group must make changes to keep all group members motivated and working toward the same goal.

Checkup: Contracts and Partnership Agreements

Most people read legal documents once and file them away. If you find yourself dissatisfied at work, you may want to appeal to your partnership agreement or contract to remedy certain issues. On the other hand, it may be time to admit that the partnership agreement no longer provides what you want. In either case, pull out your contract or agreement, and consider the following questions:

1. Which of the following agreements governs your practice setting:

   A. Employment contract

   B. Written partnership agreement

   C. Oral partnership agreement

2. If your partnership agreement is oral, what mechanisms are in place for resolving disputes?

3. If your partnership agreement is oral, how amenable are your partners to creating a written document?

4. Do you understand how compensation is calculated according to your partnership agreement or contract? Can you state the formula in your own words?

5. Do you understand how expenses are classified and shared under your agreement? Is there a difference in practice?

6. How is the managing partner compensated? Does the compensation formula as written make sense to you? Is there any difference in how it is applied in practice?

7. How are shares in the equity of the practice assigned by contract? Have the partners reviewed the amounts and the procedure since the practice was established?

8. If a partner leaves the practice, how does the practice buy back the partner's shares of the practice? Is the language of the agreement clear about the procedure?

9. How does the partnership agreement structure the management of the practice? Who serves on the governing committee or board of directors?

10. If you are now contemplating a career change, have you had a lawyer who specializes in health law read your partnership agreement and advise you on how to make the career change you envision?

How to Get Out Gracefully

Where We Are

In Part I, you began to explore your psychological readiness for making a major change in your career and in your life. You also examined your legal situation and how your practice is structured, which may factor heavily in your plan of action.

Where We Are Headed

Now that you have framed the question and laid out some options, you will want to assess your financial, legal, and psychological situations more closely. Part II includes two chapters on financial planning. The first focuses on the basics of money — how to set goals and how to make the best use of assets. The second chapter in this part centers on managing your finances through a transition and setting up a new financial plan to guarantee financial independence. The remaining chapters look at the legal and insurance issues to consider when you leave your practice and how to smoothly transition into your new career.

Chapter 3

Financial Planning to Ease Your Exit

Joel M Blau, CFP and Ronald J Paprocki, JD, CFP

O nce you make the decision to leave your practice, a multitude of other decisions will follow. Before you can answer them all, you must first determine what you will be doing next. Will you join another practice? Become a sole practitioner? Work in another field? Or will you simply stop working? Each of these choices involves a number of financial considerations that center on cash flow and income tax implications.

Investment and Financial Planning Preliminaries

When constructing a financial plan, many physicians complain about the overwhelming (and often conflicting) amount of information available. This information, combined with the numerous strategies suggested by a variety of professionals, often produces a paralysis that results in nothing being accomplished.

We find that the best way to avoid this paralysis is to break the plan down into small steps that are easily completed. The first step is to determine the appropriate process of building your financial plan—a plan for the plan.

When constructing your financial plan, picture the pyramids of Egypt. Pyramids are built on a solid large base. As they rise into the sky, they begin to narrow until reaching the apex. This basic design has enabled the Egyptian pyramids to withstand the test of time over thousands of years. Would the Egyptians have had the same results if they had started with the apex at the bottom and the large base on top? Of course not—but this appears to be the investment architecture used by many physicians every day.

The First Step: Hazard Protection

The pyramid is the model for your financial plan. Consider the base to be the fundamental strategy of your financial plan and the apex to be the investment you will consider only after all of the previous strategies have been successfully completed (see Figure 3.1). The key is to build a strong foundation that will act as your pyramid's base. This base should address the most fundamental of all of your financial matters, and it should focus on the most important asset in your possession.

Figure 3.1: The Financial-Planning Pyramid

Planning Your Plan: The Financial-Planning Pyramid

Speculation

Tax Shelters

Illiquid Investments
(tax-qualified plans,
tax-advantaged investments)

Liquid Investments
(easily converted to cash)

Emergency Funds
(3-6 months after-tax living expenses)

Hazard Protection
(lawsuits, disability, death)

Most physicians believe that their most important asset is their ability to work in their profession. Now that you are considering altering your current employment status, you may need to rethink this question. After all, earlier in your career you might have been able to lose financial assets and still be able to replace them. Now, though, you may be deciding to reduce or end your income-earning activities. If this is the case, you may need to consider the value of your financial holdings as the truly most important asset in your possession. The foundation of your financial plan should address this most valuable asset. Let's call this section of the pyramid "hazard protection."

When you completed your residency, who was the first financial advisor to contact you? Was it a stockbroker or a municipal bond broker? Probably not. Why? Because at that point in your career you had not accumulated enough excess investment dollars to generate commissions for these financial salespeople. The odds are that your first contact was with an insurance agent. The agent probably talked about the effect your premature death or disability would have on your family. He probably explained that your most important asset was your ability to earn income and that you must insure against that loss.

This does make a great deal of sense. Early in their careers, physicians have an excellent "economic life value." This means that the present value of expected earnings is quite high. For example, the economic life value of a physician expected to earn $150,000 per year for thirty-five years is approximately $3,795,427.* No doubt a very valuable asset. (See Figure 3.2.)

Now, as your career plans are changing, you need to do as much as possible to protect the income-producing power of the assets that you have accumulated. The income produced by these assets can support you and your spouse for the remainder of your lives.

What can have an impact on this most important asset at your stage of life? There are two main factors: a successful lawsuit brought against you or an extended illness that requires substantial nursing-home care.

---

* Adjusted for 4% inflation and a 6% rate of return.

Figure 3.2: Physicians' Economic Life Values

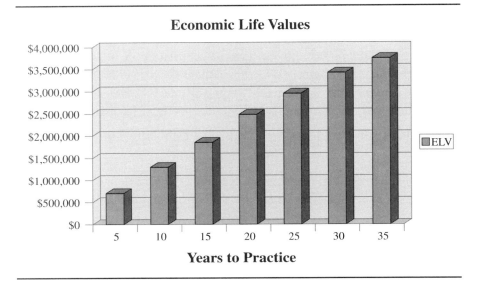

For example, a long-term illness can easily generate monthly expenses of $5,000 to $10,000. At that rate, the assets you have spent a lifetime accumulating can be depleted quickly. A lawsuit will bring into plan another aspect of hazard protection, shielding the assets that you have been able to accumulate over time. Asset protection is a growing area of the law and is critical to address for effective financial planning.

Another aspect of hazard protection is estate planning. Regardless of your current income or the size of your estate, you must make decisions today that will affect your family in the future. If you have children, you must name guardians and trustees. You should put your postmortem desires in writing about how assets should be treated and who should receive particular assets at your death.

You may be thinking that a solid foundation is not the exciting entry into financial planning that you may have imagined. Laying a foundation can be tedious, and let's face it, who wants to think about hazards and death while an exciting new dimension to your life is just beginning? Because this can be a stressful and somewhat time-consuming task, many physicians simply ignore the base and head straight for the apex—those speculative investments that promise spectacular returns and tax write-offs. It is not until it is too late that they realize why a pyramid is built from the base up.

The Second Step: Emergency Funds

After setting down a sound foundation, you should build a layer of cash reserves. *Cash reserves* include those assets with principals that do not fluctuate in value, funds that are available daily. You simply walk into the bank, visit the local automated teller machine, or write a check to access these funds. This category includes checking and savings accounts, money market accounts, and short-term certificates of deposit. Cash reserves provide necessary emergency funds.

The risk/reward tradeoff for cash reserves is that these low-risk vehicles usually provide the lowest interest rates and thus do not offer meaningful growth potential. You want to have cash available in case the car breaks down, the roof needs a repair, or you have a month when expenses exceed income. The dollar amount to be kept in an emergency fund depends on your personal situation.

A fully-funded emergency reserve is necessary, as the worst time to sell any investment—stocks, bonds, or real estate—is when you must. To determine an appropriate funding level, you should take a close look at your average monthly living expenses. This exercise can be accomplished simply by adding up the amount of checks that you wrote over a one-month period from your checkbook register. Using two or three months will give you a better idea of your average monthly expenses. Don't forget to include a portion of your large bills that may only be paid yearly such as insurance premiums, property taxes, and home improvements.

Your total average monthly expense is also known as your *standard of living*. Although everyone's standard of living is different, the guidelines are similar. Financial planning practitioners recommend that an emergency fund should equal approximately three times your monthly living expenses. This is an adequate amount assuming that your income is predictable and consistent. If, on the other hand, you are a sole practitioner and your monthly income is more erratic, you may want to have as much as six times your average monthly total living expenses allocated to cash equivalents.

In addition to this monthly living expense amount, we often suggest that households include in an emergency fund the amount of expected expenses scheduled to occur within the next three to six months. After all, the sale of an investment asset at an inopportune time can be extremely expensive, and may force you to suffer a loss you did not expect.

Because cash equivalents by definition earn relatively low rates of return, many physicians chose another alternative that frees up more of their cash for investments. A homeowner can establish an equity line of credit against the value of the residence. In this alternative, you receive a checkbook that enables you to write checks against your home equity, but interest is paid only on the actual amount used. In addition, the interest paid on the loan is generally deductible on a personal tax return. This strategy works if you have the necessary equity available in your home. The disadvantage is that even though the interest is deductible, you must still repay the loan and you incur the interest expense.

Because another objective of an emergency fund is peace of mind, it is important that you choose the method you are most comfortable with based on your lifestyle. Keep in mind that just as an underfunded reserve can force you to dip into longer-term savings vehicles, an overfunded reserve reduces your ability to invest in other vehicles that may offer greater returns in the long run.

The Third Step: Liquid Investments

As you continue to climb the financial planning pyramid, you will reach the level of liquid investments. *Liquid investments* are those investments that can be sold and converted to cash within seven to ten days. Liquid investments will show some fluctuation of principal. Thus, at the time of sale, the value of a liquid investment can be more or less than the original investment. So even though the return of principal is not guaranteed, you can receive the proceeds in a timely fashion. Examples of liquid investments are stocks, bonds, and mutual funds. Also included could be cash values of variable-life insurance policies. However, depending on the insurance company, it can take longer than seven to ten days to liquidate.

Unlike cash reserves, liquid investments have the advantage of higher potential returns over time, but along with this potential comes fluctuation or risk. There is nothing wrong with taking on increased risk, as long as you have an adequate emergency fund to give you needed protection.

The Fourth Step: Illiquid Assets

Continuing your ascent of the financial-planning pyramid, you reach the level of *illiquid investments*. We categorize these investments into two basic types: tax-qualified plans and tax-advantaged investments. Included in the first category are qualified retirement plans, including pensions, profit sharing, self-employed plans (SEPs), SIMPLE plans, Keoghs, and individual retirement accounts (IRAs). The investments in these plans may be in cash equivalents, stocks, bonds, mutual funds, or other types of investments. As a general rule, these funds are somewhat illiquid until age $59^1/_2$. Withdrawals from these plans before age $59^1/_2$ are typically assessed a 10% IRS penalty and are considered taxable income in the year received.

The second category includes annuities. Once again, there can be substantial penalties for early withdrawal. Penalties notwithstanding, there are a number of advantages in a illiquid investment that cannot be duplicated in other types of investments. In the case of qualified plans and annuities, interest, dividends, and capital gains grow on a tax-deferred basis. Qualified plans such as SEPs and IRAs have the added advantage of tax-deductible contributions. This saves you tax dollars while you are in your peak earning years.

The Fifth Step: Tax Shelters

As you near the top of the pyramid, you reach the level of *tax shelters*. Tax shelters were popular with physicians in the early 1980s. These investments were originally sold as a way to lower income tax liability while also providing growth or income potential. Vehicles used as shelters included real estate, equipment leasing, movie production, and even jojoba fields.

Tax shelters are extremely illiquid. Many physicians bought into these programs not only because of the tax benefits but also because of the viability of the actual investment. In 1986, however, the tax law changed, taking away many of the tax advantages. In addition, many of the underlying investment vehicles did not perform up to expectations. Tax shelters and limited partnerships are still available in the market today, but the empha-sis has shifted from tax benefits to the economic soundness of the invest-ment itself. Tax shelters must make good economic sense to you before you make a long-term commitment.

The Apex: Speculation

The apex of the financial planning pyramid is reserved for the highest-risk investments. These investments typically have high return potential as well as high loss potential. Included in this category are commodities futures trading and venture capital opportunities. Commodities futures trading involves the use of leverage to buy or sell futures contracts in precious metals, grains, meats, currencies, and stock and bond market indices. With these investments, leverage and the use of margin accounts have created the potential to actually lose more than the original investment.

Venture capital is used to finance a new or expanding business. This cate-gory includes money that you may lend to a relative or friend to start a business. On the surface, these investments may appear to be viable, but in reality, the majority of times you will lose not only your money but your friend as well. If you lend money to a relative, the situation can be even worse because you cannot stop being related.

The financial-planning pyramid should be considered whenever you make an investment decision. Being aware of the risk-reward trade-off, and where a given investment fits into you own planning pyramid, will enable you to avoid common mistakes. You must keep in mind that generally, you do not get something worthwhile for nothing. There is no perfect invest-ment that will give you high guaranteed returns without incurring any risks. With this basic understanding in mind, you should also realize that each individual's pyramid will be structured differently based on individ-ual risk tolerance and long-term objectives.

An analysis of many physicians' portfolios shows an overwhelming amount of apex investments, such as limited partnerships, venture capital, and other highly leveraged investments. However, what is interesting is that these under-performing investments are not usually the reason many physicians are not financially independent. The most common reason is pure and simple procrastination. Most Americans are financial planning procrastinators, and physicians are no exception. The most frustrating part of our job is telling a fifty-year-old physician making $200,000 per year that he or she needs to save $225,000 annually to accomplish newly defined retirement goals. This is a common problem with a simple solution. The key element in long-term savings is time. The sooner you begin to set aside funds for any long-term goal, whether it is retirement, college education, or a new home, the easier it is to accomplish that goal. Figure 3.2 illustrates the financial-planning pyramid paramount to a successful financial future.

Your Qualified Retirement Plan

Qualified retirement plans generally constitute the major portion of a physician's investment portfolio as well as their overall net worth. The term *qualified retirement* plan is defined as one that is congressionally approved and has the following major tax benefits:

- The employer's contribution can be deducted for income tax purposes (Internal Revenue Code Section 404 (a)).

- Contributions are currently not taxable to the employee (Internal Revenue Code Section 402 (a) and 403 (a)).

- The earnings on the plan's investment accumulate on a tax-deferred basis (Internal Revenue Code Section 501 (a)).

Included in this category would be profit sharing plans, 401(k) plans, and various pension plans. We discuss in detail the various plans' advantages and disadvantages in Chapter 8. For now we simply need to distinguish between the two major types of qualified retirement plans and the steps you will need to take when leaving a practice.

Retirement plans will either be categorized as "defined benefit" or "defined contribution." Defined benefit plans define and quantify the benefit amount each participant will receive at a given age. Actuarial calculations are used to determine how much may be contributed for each participant. Because this plan is essentially a promise of a future benefit of retirement income, the assets generally will not be available to the participant until attainment of a certain age and/or a minimal number of years of service to the employer. Some plans, however, will allow distributions to begin earlier, but at a substantially reduced benefit.

Experience indicates that defined benefit plans are becoming far less popular over time. Many large employers, such as hospitals or large clinics, may still offer such plans. Smaller practices have seemed to move away from defined benefit plans due to their inherent complexity and unknown contribution commitment. If you are a participant in such a plan, check with your pension administrator to determine the distribution options available to you. At that point, you can assess its impact on your future financial resources and needs. The administrator can tell you the income payouts available at various ages or whether a lump sum distribution option is also available. A "lump sum" distribution is the distribution of a retirement plan participant's entire account balance. The distribution of the entire account balance enables the participant to assume a much more active role in the investment management of the funds and enables the participant complete control over the use of the funds. (See "Distributions from Your Plan Retirement Income," later in this chapter for a discussion of the income tax issues of lump sum distributions.)

Defined contribution plans, on the other hand, do not promise a certain dollar amount at retirement. Rather, the employer contributes assets each year that are invested for the participant's benefit. Whatever that dollar amount grows to is what the participant is entitled. Certain defined contributions plans, such as a 401(k) plan, enable participants to contribute additional funds.

Another factor relating to your retirement plan is the plan's "vesting schedule." This schedule dictates how much of your retirement account funded by employer contributions you will be able to keep upon your departure. Be sure to check with the pension administrator to determine the impact service termination has on your plan assets. They will be able to inform you of your balance as well as the length of time further required to attain 100% vesting. Most plans use graduated, or "cliff" vesting schedules, which provide an increase to the vesting schedule with each year of employment. It is critical to have this information. You may find that staying on an additional 4 months may make the difference between receiving your total account value versus only 50% or 80% of that amount.

Practice Alert: Saving Now For Retirement

Saving for retirement comes up early in this book. Why? As mentioned, for many people, the assets in retirement accounts form their largest single set of holdings. Further, the importance of Social Security is declining relative to other retirement plans, which have become increasingly flexible. Finally, there is the "miracle" of compounding—especially if you take advantage of its long-term, highly profitable effects. All of these factors mean that the time to begin planning and saving for retirement is now.

Transferring Plan Assets

If your decision is to work elsewhere, either in a medical or even non-medical field, you should inquire as to the types of retirement plans available. Certain qualified retirement plans enable retirement plan assets from a previous plan to be "rolled over" into their plan. The term "rollover" refers to the process of transferring your retirement plan account into another tax-qualified plan, without incurring current income taxation.

This alternative also enables the existing plan assets to be transferred to a separate IRA. Just because an employer allows rollovers from new employees to be added to their plan, doing so may not be in your best interest. For example, the investment alternative in the new plan may not be as interesting as those available in a separate IRA. Some retirement accounts are "self directed," meaning that you decide the investment vehicles to be used. If not "self directed," the trustees have pre-selected the investment managers. These selections may not fit your investment plan. With an IRA, you always have the ability to select your own investment managers or advisors, based on your own goals and objectives. Once you have made that decision, care must be taken in how you actually transfer your account elsewhere.

Withholding Taxes on Your Retirement Account

Current tax law requires that retirement plans withhold 20% of plan assets when payments are made directly to a former plan participant. This withholding is done for income tax purposes. Participants have the opportunity to roll the pre-tax amount of the plan distribution into a new employer's retirement plan or an IRA rollover. However, the participant must find the funds that were withheld from the distribution if the full amount is not placed in the IRA or employer plans, then the participant is deemed to have taken a distribution equal to the amount not placed in the IRA. This results in an income tax liability and an additional 10% penalty tax if the participant is younger than 59^1/$_2$.

This tax problem can be avoided by requesting a trustee-to-trustee transfer of your retirement account. No taxes will be withheld, and you have no concerns for possible penalty taxes.

Avoiding the Early Retirement Penalty

As a general rule, distributions from qualified plans are subject to a 10% penalty tax if they are withdrawn prior to the participant reaching age 59^1/$_2$, becoming disabled, or dying. The term "qualified plan" includes pensions, profit sharing plans, SEPs, Keoghs, IRAs, and 403(b) annuities. Additionally, withdrawals are subject to ordinary income taxation. This reduces a premature distribution even further. But what happens if your financial situation upon leaving a practice requires you to access those plan assets before age 59^1/$_2$?

When the age 59^1/$_2$ rule was enacted, a general assumption was made that a "normal" minimum retirement age would be 60 years of age. But times have changed! Corporate downsizing has forced many professionals to begin retirement in their mid-50s. Many physicians look at health care reform and consider retiring before the magic age of 59^1/$_2$. Can you access retirement funds without paying the 10% penalty? Depending upon your personal situation and potential need for the funds, there are several possible exceptions to the penalty rule.

If your objective is simply early retirement, the IRS will waive the 10% penalty if the distribution is part of a scheduled series of substantially equal payments.

There are three different approved methods when calculating these types of distributions:

- **Single or Joint Life Expectancy.** This method spreads payments over the number of years set forth in the IRS tables based on a single life, or joint life which includes your named beneficiary.

- **Amortization.** Using this method, payments are similar to the annual amount required to pay off a loan at a reasonable interest rate over your life expectancy.

- **Annuity.** This method uses an annuity factor which has been determined from a reasonable mortality table utilizing a given interest rate assumption. Once you begin annual distributions, you must continue them until age $59\frac{1}{2}$, or five years, whichever is later. Under this rule, a 55-year-old may receive fixed annual distributions until age 60. At that time, the fixed distribution can be stopped and the recipient can begin to take out as little or as much as needed from the qualified plan at their own discretion (IRC Section 72t).

Even though all three methods may seem similar, each requires different annual distributions. If you are considering using the "Substantially Equal Payments" exception, have your accountant determine each method's results in order to match your income needs and avoid additional income taxation.

The Tax Payer Relief Act of 1997 provided additional opportunities to avoid the 10% early withdrawal penalty. An IRA withdrawal without penalty is now allowed for the acquisition of a first home, up to a limit of $10,000. Penalty free withdrawals are also allowed for money used to pay qualified higher education expenses for the taxpayer, the spouse, children, or grandchildren. Other exceptions include payment of certain medical expenses and payment of health insurance premiums for the unemployed. As always, the 10% premature withdrawal penalty is waived for distributions made at the death or disability of the participant.

Your situation may not require that you tap into your IRA early. Because there has been tremendous growth of assets within qualified plans, it is not surprising that a significant portion of a physician's total portfolio may consist of tax-deferred assets. As often happens at retirement, those qualified plan assets are rolled into an IRA for the benefit of the participant. When the time comes to begin withdrawals from an IRA, the income tax consequences can become substantial.

Distributions from Your Plan Retirement Income

Distributions from an IRA can be received free of penalty as early as age $59^1/_2$, but must begin no later than April 1 of the year following the year in which the participant turns $70^1/_2$. Not only does the government require distributions to be made, it also determines the minimum amount that must be withdrawn annually.

In order to minimize current income tax liability and enable the IRA to continue to grow tax deferred, participants are allowed to take a "required minimum" distribution. The amount of this distribution is determined actuarially by using the life expectancy of the participant and the beneficiary. The distribution rate can be fixed at the time of the required beginning date, or by recalculating the minimum distribution based upon life expectancies at that time.

Recently, proposed regulations regarding required minimum distributions have been published (REG-130477-00; REG-130481-00). These proposed regulations simplify what has been one of the most complex areas of tax law regarding retirement. This is important, as for most physicians, qualified retirement plans and IRAs make up a large percentage of their net worth.

What has changed is the process by which retirees decide how their required minimum distribution will be calculated. Required minimum distributions will now actually be lower, as the new tables automatically assume a joint life expectancy with the beneficiary being 10 years younger than the participant, even if he or she isn't. If a spouse is the beneficiary and the age spread is greater than 10 years, you benefit from another table that lowers mandatory distributions based on actual joint life expectancy.

In addition, the IRS is providing greater post-death planning opportunities for executors by allowing the naming of a beneficiary and contingent beneficiary up to the end of the year following the year of death. The old rules made a beneficiary designation irrevocable at the time of death. Not naming a beneficiary usually resulted in a payout of the account over five years. Now, a beneficiary can be identified after death, with distributions being made over their lifetime.

So why would the IRS take such a monumental step to lower required minimum distributions thus decreasing the amount of taxes owed? Many feel that with all of the complex choices available, the IRS was simply unable to audit the activity. Now the IRS will require the plan's custodian, such as a brokerage firm or bank, to report the minimum distribution.

While final regulations are not expected to be implemented until January 1, 2002, the IRS is allowing taxpayers to use either the old or the new proposed regulations in figuring required minimum distributions for 2001. If you are locked into an unfavorable payout strategy, take advantage of opportunities provided by the new rules.

The table used for determining the most required minimum distributions is shown in Table 3.1. Once again, this table is used unless the spouse beneficiary is more than 10 years younger than the participant.

Table 3.1: The Uniform Table

Tables for Determining Applicable Divisor					
Age	Applicable divisor	Age	Applicable divisor	Age	Applicable divisor
70	26.2	86	13.1	102	5.0
71	25.3	87	12.4	103	4.7
72	24.4	88	11.8	104	4.4
73	23.5	89	11.1	105	4.1
74	22.7	90	10.5	106	3.8
75	21.8	91	9.9	107	3.6
76	20.9	92	9.4	108	3.3
77	20.1	93	8.8	109	3.1
78	19.2	94	8.3	110	2.8
79	18.4	95	7.8	111	2.6
80	17.6	96	7.3	112	2.4
81	16.8	97	6.9	113	2.2
82	16.0	98	6.5	114	2.0
83	15.3	99	6.1	115+	1.8
84	14.5	100	5.7		
85	13.8	101	5.3		

One form of distribution from a retirement plan is a "lump sum" distribution from your plan. This results in a single payment from your plan. Some individuals are allowed special tax treatment on lump sum contributions. If the taxpayer was age 50 or older on January 1, 1986, he or she can:

- Pay the tax at capital gains rates on the pre-1974 portion and at ordinary income rates for the post 1973 portion, or

- Elect ten-year averaging for the post-1973 portion or the entire amount.

If the previous special situations sound confusing, there is an alternative that is available to everyone regardless of age. Lump sum distributions from qualified plans may be transferred to a Rollover IRA. No tax is due at the time of transfer, however distributions are taxed as ordinary income. This enables you to withdraw just the amount you need and let the rest of the account continue to grow on a tax-deferred basis.

The vast majority of retirees bypass lump-sum withdrawal in favor of the rollover as it enables you to control the amount and timing of withdrawals based on monthly retirement income needs. Keep in mind that distributions must begin by April 1 following the year in which you reach at $70^1/_2$, no matter what kind of qualified plan you own.

Once the decision is made to leave your current practice, you will need to determine how to continue an income stream. If you are gong to work somewhere else at a similar income, it is probably not a concern. One the other hand, if you accept employment at a lower income level, you need to quantify your monthly standard of living. If your new income is below your standard of living, you have just two options: lower your standard of living, or supplement your earned income.

Checkup: Do You Have a Five-Year Plan?

Many people find that making a five-year plan is a good exercise. Planning focuses you on your immediate objectives and how you can make them unfold over time. You can catch a glimpse of how decisions today may work out in a year or two. At the same time, a five-year plan that you compile yourself is flexible. You can add your own ideas and account for outside factors at any time.

To begin putting together a five-year plan, fill in the years in the grid that follows, beginning with the current year. Under *Career,* list plans and aspirations for your career. Do you foresee increased number of patients? A change in specialty? New training? A Sabbatical? Think about where you would like to be in your career five years from now.

Under *Financial,* write down goals and plans that relate to your personal finances. Would you like to buy a house next year? Are you planning to sell your condominium in two years? Have you set up a retirement plan, and what goals have you put in place for your plan? What would you like your net worth to amount to five years from now?

The column titled *Practice Setting* is the place for management decisions about your medical partnership or corporation. Will you change the structure of your partnership in the next few years? Is your current status as an employee of a health plan—and are you satisfied with the arrangement? What plans would you have to make to open your own office? You may want to list them step by step.

Year	Career	Financial	Practice Setting
Year 1 (current) _____			
Year 2 _____			
Year 3 _____			
Year 4 _____			
Year 5 _____			

Self-Test: Building a Pyramid

A pyramid is a good metaphor for personal finances. In this self-test, you will work from the base to the apex. Focus on the lower levels in particular so that you can assess how solidly your assets are structured. Younger doctors probably will have few investments near the top of the pyramid. If you find that your portfolio of assets is top-heavy, or that you have all of your investments at the speculative apex, it may be time to rethink your investment strategy.

The Base: Hazard Protection

1. Do you put money in savings or investments regularly?

2. Have you taken on an adequate amount of life insurance to protect your family in the event of your death?

3. Is your partnership agreement written so that your assets are sheltered from the actions of your partners or the failure of the partnership? Similarly, if you have incorporated, how is your corporation structured to protect your personal assets? In general, what have you done to limit your liability?

4. Do you have an estate plan in place?

The Second Step: Cash Reserves

1. Have you taken time to calculate your monthly household expenses?

2. How much cash do you have on hand to run your practice?

3. How much money do you typically keep in your household checking account? Business checking account?

4. Do you keep an emergency reserve accessible in savings accounts, money-market accounts, and short-term certificates of deposit? How much?

5. How much credit-card debt do you carry, and how much does your credit-card debt affect your monthly budget and your emergency reserve?

The Third Step: Liquid Investments

1. Have you invested in stocks? Which stocks have you chosen? How much are your stocks currently worth and how often do you invest in stocks?

2. Have you invested in bonds? Which bonds have you chosen? How much is your portfolio of bonds worth, and how often do you make investments in it?

3. Have you invested in mutual funds? Which mutual funds have you chosen? How much are your mutual funds worth, and how often do you invest in them?

4. Do you have a financial advisor? What sources of information and advice do you rely on for making investments?

The Fourth Step: Illiquid Assets

1. How is your retirement plan structured?

2. Have you funded an annuity?

The Fifth Step: Tax Shelters

1. Have you made an investment that would qualify as a tax shelter?

2. How did you learn about the tax shelter? Whose advice did you rely on? Do you understand how the tax shelter is structured and how it lowers your tax liability?

The Apex: High-Risk Investing

1. Have you opened an account with a commodities futures trading company? How did you find out about the company? What is the company's investment strategy? What return can you reasonably expect?

2. Have you contributed venture capital to a startup business? How did you assess the viability of the startup? What return can you reasonably expect?

Chapter 4

Twin Goals: Career Change and Future Financial Independence

Joel M Blau, CFP and Ronald J Paprocki, JD, CFP

Personal conflicts with partners have caused many physicians to consider breaking up a medical practice. Conflict occurs most often when the partners have mismatched goals. For example, one partner may want to work very hard for long hours to compensate for a dropping income, while another may be preparing for retirement, winding down, or simply wants to work at a less hectic pace and is willing to accept a lower income. This situation appears to happen most often with physicians of widely differing ages. The 60-year-old partner may have had his home for 25 years with little or no mortgage remaining, children's college funding has probably ended, and he or she has enjoyed many expensive vacations. This partner's sole goal at this point of life is simply to maintain the assets that have been accumulated through the years and, with proper management, watch these investments grow. This stance is in stark contrast to a 40-year-old partner struggling to make ends meet with relatively large mortgage payments, auto leases, savings for children's future education costs, and payments on old student loans.

To give you flexibility and choices, you should start planning for your own financial independence. *Financial independence* refers to your ability to maintain your desired lifestyle without having to work. Attainment of financial independence will provide you with peace of mind as well as many options for your future. Financial independence can enable you to

switch careers and accept a lower income, continue working at a less rigorous pace, or simply enjoy an early retirement.

Financial independence does not happen by chance. It is something you
must work toward from the early stages of your medical career. Wouldn't
it be great to be at a point where you feel that you actually have choices in
life relative to your career? Unfortunately, many physicians simply do not
feel that they have that luxury. Physicians, more often than not, feel
trapped within their practice, whether from the cost and time involved in
buying into the practice or those important paychecks that enable the
lifestyle to which their families have become accustomed.

From a financial standpoint, doctors are not immune to financial disaster,
and a physician in financial disarray and distress can have a dramatic
impact on colleagues. Financial problems occur for many reasons, including spending more than income earned, poor investing, divorce, as well as
other family situations such as higher than expected expenses for children's needs and assisting other family members. Conflict can occur as
one physician is trying to dig himself out of a hole. It is not uncommon to
see drastic attempts to decrease costs by reducing the amount of staff support while attempting to see more patients. This stress is also passed
through to the other physicians in the practice regardless of their own
financial status, thus causing additional partner conflict and unhappiness in
a working environment.

Taking Time for Financial Education

Most physicians are either unable or unwilling to examine the feasibility of
future financial independence. This problem has existed from the beginning of your medical training. As a student, you attended a fine university
for many years. You achieved the highest undergraduate grades to move on
to medical school where you studied day and night to acquire your knowledge. Only after several grueling years were you finally ready to enter the
workforce. Even at that point, some of you chose to continue your education and training in a specialty field.

When the time finally came to begin your career, you found yourself heavily in debt. Maybe you had student loans that were beginning to come due.

Maybe you had spent your savings, grants, and parents' money to reach your current state—temporarily unemployed. You knew, though, that once your professional career began, you could look forward to being one of the highest paid professionals in your community as well as in the country. These paychecks may have been in addition to quarterly practice bonuses sufficient to buy a new car or even help with a down payment on a house.

As your practice of medicine grew, you found that you were able to save money regularly. What would you do with those extra funds? What *should* you do with those funds to ensure your family's well-being in the event you wanted to stop working or were physically or mentally unable to continue working?

If these were medically-related questions, you would have the answers. You could refer back to a class or specific textbook that would relate to your inquiry. You could contact a colleague and bounce the questions off of him or her. Maybe the answers were in a book in your office. Wherever the answers might be found, you could find them.

But these are not medical questions. They are financial-planning questions, and when it comes to making financial decisions, how educated are you? How many courses did you take in business administration? Did you attend the lectures in Finance 101 or the class on basic investments? How many hours did you take in personal risk management and estate tax planning? The fact is that you could not take these classes because you were too busy concentrating on your medical degree. For this reason, you must get a handle on personal financial planning strategies that will enable you to attain true financial independence.

Golf courses, tennis courts, and the doctors' lounge are great places for unsolicited financial advice. Every day you hear about a hot stock that was bought and then doubled within a month or the story about the doctor who says he can retire at age 45 or 50. You cannot understand how your friends have the time and the financial savvy to be so involved in their own financial plans. It seems that you are hearing one success story after another.

What you never seem to hear are the financial horror stories: the stock that plummeted the week after your neighbor bought it on a "hot" tip or the bond that was supposed to pay much higher than average dividends, but these dividends in fact were never paid because the company declared bankruptcy. There are more stories of lost money and lost dreams than success stories, but you probably will not hear many of these stories in the lounge. Who among us wants to look foolish?

You cannot buy a mutual fund or stock just because your colleague bought it. His or her long-term goals and objectives may be, and probably are, different from yours. The key is to control your own destiny through a comprehensive understanding of financial strategies and techniques to attain true financial independence that will enable you to leave your practice when *you* want to. Only by understanding these strategies and techniques will you be able to make the best decisions for you and your family.

Consulting with physicians daily, we often find ourselves to be the bearer of bad news. We have to tell clients that they will not be able to retire at their desired income level. However, proper planning now will enable you to avoid bad news. The answer is neither to spend all your money today nor is it to save everything for the future.

Guaranteeing Financial Independence

As the saying goes, "People don't plan to fail, they fail to plan." There never seems to be a good time to begin to plan. "Maybe next year when the house is paid off… Only two more years until the kids are through with school… After my daughter's wedding, then I'll be able to save for retirement…" And so it goes. The excuses are endless, but the reality is that you must begin to plan for your financial future today.

Successful financial planning requires three key elements:

- Setting clear goals
- Maximizing tax benefits
- Exercising discipline

Set Clear Goals

Ask yourself these basic questions: When do you plan to retire or achieve financial independence? Will you be most likely to retire completely, or will you continue to do something to generate income? What are your overall income objectives for retirement? Answers to these and similar questions should provide you with the foundation on which to build your retirement plan. When thinking about goals, be sure to consider the questions in Table 4.1 as they relate to your own situation.

Table 4.1: Determine Your Goals

EDUCATION	ESTATE PLANNING
Current need?	Who should receive?
Inflation?	Can costs be avoided?
Percentage of cost to cover?	Are management skills required?
Sources of capital?	Will taxes be excessive?
RISK MANAGEMENT	**INVESTMENTS**
Surviving family income needs?	What risks are you taking?
Time to provide income?	What are your expectations?
Source of income?	Are tax strategies being optimized?
RETIREMENT	
When?	Rates of return?
Income objective?	Sources of income?

Take Stock of Retirement Assets

What benefits can you expect from your retirement plans? Should you count on Social Security? As you continue to pay into the Social Security system, you should be aware of the realities that face the future of the program.

Fifty years ago there were approximately 42 workers contributing to the Social Security system for every retiree collecting a benefit. Today there are only 3.3 workers for every beneficiary. Projections indicate that by the year 2025 the ratio will have dropped to 2.2 workers per retiree. In just over 15 years, the amount of money going out in benefits will surpass the amount coming in. (All statistics are from Social Security Administration Publication No. 05-10055.) While legislators discuss various options to save the system, we can almost be assured that the outcome will involve higher taxes for working Americans, changes in accepted retirement ages, and lower benefits for at least some retirees.

For many individuals, the "normal" retirement age has already been raised. Those born before 1942 can draw full benefits at age 65. For those born between 1943 and 1959, the normal retirement age to receive 100% of benefits has been raised to 66. If you were born after 1959, you will have to wait until age 75 before you can collect full benefits. Retirees can begin collecting reduced benefits at age 62. This payout will equal 80% of the projected full annual benefit. A 63-year-old who decides to begin receiving benefits will receive an 86.6% payout, while a 64-year-old retiree will collect 93.3% of the full benefit.

The financial strength of the Social Security system seems spectacular when compared to the Medicare system. While the system has been barely breaking even, a deficit of $35 billion is projected for 1999. The Medicare Board of Trustees believes that if something is not done now to reduce Medicare spending, the system is likely to be bankrupt early in the twenty-first century.

Maximize Tax Benefits

An easy way to think of tax benefits is to realize that there are three distinct phases of an investment: the deposit or purchase phase, the accumulation or growth phase, and the liquidation phase. The government allows, at best, a tax benefit to be available in two of the three phases. For example, retirement plan contributions are tax deductible and accumulate on a tax-deferred basis, but withdrawals are taxed at ordinary income-tax rates. Other investments, such as municipal bonds, are purchased on an after-tax basis and accumulate tax free, and the income generated is received on a federally tax-free basis. As of now, there are no investments that allow for tax-deductible contributions, tax-free growth, and tax-free income. Consider these different phases and do as much as possible to receive the tax benefits to which you are entitled.

Exercise Discipline

All of the retirement and tax-planning strategies in the world will not provide you with benefits if you do not actually implement your plans. It is important to understand that you not only need to gather information to make informed decisions, but you also must act on those decisions. The earlier you begin, the greater the chance you will enjoy a financially successful retirement. The key to a financially secure retirement is not just to plan, but to act.

Take Advantage of Compound Interest

No discussion involving potentially leaving your practice can be complete without an understanding of how compound interest works, the benefits of compounding, and the erosion of income due to taxes and inflation.

Many investment vehicles have an income component. Income can be derived from interest (bank savings accounts, certificates of deposit, and bonds), dividends (common stock and mutual funds), or capital gains distributions (mutual funds). In the case of bank accounts and mutual funds, you have the option of either receiving your income in the form of a check every month (or whenever distributed) or reinvesting the income in the original investment. The latter is referred to as *compounding*.

When you leave a practice you may find that you are in need of current income and will have no choice but to receive income distributions. On the other hand, if you do not currently need the income due to other employment opportunities, you should consider compounding. Compounding can cause great increases on your actual returns. Consider for a moment a $100,000 bank certificate of deposit paying an annual interest rate of 6%. If you choose to take the income as a monthly distribution, you will receive $6,000 a year ($100,000 x 0.06), or $500 a month. If, on the other hand, you choose to compound each month, you will earn $6,168. This figure, in effect, is a yield of 6.168% and highlights the difference between the terms *rate* and *yield*.

Interestingly, if you were to double the rate of return to 12%, taken as a distribution, the income would be $12,000. If the amount were left to compound, the actual dollar return would be $12,682—an effective yield of 12.682%. As you can see, there is an exponential relationship in compounding. By simply doubling the 6% compounded rate, the dollar value rises to $12,336 (6,168 x 2). However, compounding the 12% rate increases the value of the account to $12,682, which is $346 more than simply doubling (12,682 vs 12,336). Interest is building on the interest. Compounding enables your investment dollars to work for you, instead of you working to save even more. As a general rule, if you do not need the current income generated by your investments, do not take it. Let it compound.

Picture your investments as a tank of water. As you reinvest, the tank gets more and more full. There is also a faucet attached to the tank. Turning the faucet on gives you the immediate benefit of the income. If you are not in need of current income, you simply turn the faucet off and let the compounding continue.

Unfortunately, many physicians forget the importance of compounding in their retirement years. During their working years, they compounded simply because earned income satisfied their spending needs. At retirement, they contact their brokers and investment managers and instruct them to open the faucet wide and let the income flow. But what if there is more income than needed? Extra income is no longer affected by the exponential relationship of compounding. The key is to remove only the income that is needed.

Preparing for Inflation and Taxes

In determining future income needs, you must be cognizant of those factors that work to erode hard-earned capital. Inflation, coupled with taxation, can have a devastating affect on long-term objectives.

Inflation: Avoid Capital Erosion

To illustrate the effect of inflation on your long-term goals, consider its impact on your desired monthly retirement income. Using a calculator that shows present and future values, Figure 4.1 depicts what today's 45-year-old physician can expect when retiring at age 60. The desired monthly income is $10,000 and the rate of inflation has been calculated at 4% annually.

The future value of $10,000 in 15 years at 4% inflation equals $18,009. The illustration shows that $18,009 per month will be needed at age 60 to maintain today's level of $10,000. At age 70, the monthly amount needed to equal today's $10,000 would be $26,558.

Figure 4.1: Expected Future Earnings at 4% Increase

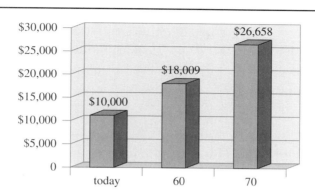

Many individuals find these numbers hard to believe. Will you have enough investment assets to generate this amount of income? If these amounts seem unrealistic, think back twenty years and consider the cost of a new car, house, and groceries. Better still, remember the price of your first house or apartment. Now think back to the last automobile you bought. Was your last car more expensive than your first home? For a great many of our clients, this is definitely true! Costs have increased dramatically over the years due to inflation. Of course, over the same twenty years, incomes have also increased. Twenty years ago, only top-level executives and professionals earned an annual income of $100,000 or more. Today, $100,000 is the annual starting pay for physicians in many parts of the country.

During our working years, we ignore the negative effect of inflation by relying on incomes increasing at levels consistent with or above inflation. Unfortunately, many of today's physicians are seeing the opposite. Incomes are dropping at a rather dramatic rate. It is not uncommon for physicians to realize that their income has peaked and their best financial years are behind them, which is why more physicians than ever are concerned about their financial futures. The days of working and letting your income and retirement plans automatically take care of themselves are over. Planning is now more important than ever, and planning for retirement income must take inflation into account. Failing to do so will be an expensive mistake. If you fail to take inflation into account, you will experience the only guarantee that we can make in the investment business: the guarantee of a continually decreasing standard of living.

Taxation: Benefits for the Careful Investor

No discussion of capital erosion can take place without mentioning income taxation. Tax rates change, sometimes increasing, sometimes decreasing. Therefore, you should incorporate tax-planning strategies in any overall financial plan and decision-making process.

Income may be taxable, tax-deferred, or tax-free, depending on the specific investment. Taxable income is reported on your IRS Form 1040. Earned income and interest are taxed at your marginal rate. Capital gains will be taxed at 20% if the investment asset was held for more than 12 months.

Deferral of investment income is most commonly accomplished through qualified retirement plans. The same is true for fixed and variable annuities. The goal is to defer the taxation of the investment income to a time in the future, such as retirement. Taxes are then paid as the funds are withdrawn, possibly at a lower rate. When combined with compounding, tax deferral can have a dramatic positive effect on your portfolio. Qualified plans have the added advantage of a tax-deductible contribution. The unknown variable is what actual tax rates will be in the future. If you have a hefty retirement income goal, you may find yourself paying taxes at the same rate as when you were working.

Tax-free investment income is limited primarily to interest generated from municipal bonds. The investor receives this income free of federal taxes. Many states also exempt municipal bond income from state taxes, further enhancing the attractiveness of the bonds. Keep in mind the risk-reward tradeoff. Because of their relative low risk and tax-free status, municipal bond interest rates are lower than interest rates for comparable corporate bonds. The determining factor will be your specific tax rate.

Although everyone wants to pay less taxes, what really matters is how much of your investment income dollars you actually keep after taxes. Very often the taxable investment proves to be the better alternative. Whenever someone suggests that you purchase a municipal bond, you should determine what the comparable taxable bond is yielding before making a decision. Often, physicians buy municipal bonds because of a personal aversion to paying income taxes, while the taxable bond may be providing a higher, after-tax yield. An added concern for retirees is that a high level of municipal-bond income can result in additional taxation of Social Security benefits.

Learning to Take Risks

Many physicians may define their risk tolerance as very conservative. They think that if the principal value of an investment fluctuates, it carries more risk than they are willing to assume. They enjoy the peace of mind in knowing that their money is being held on deposit in a simple savings account or a certificate of deposit, which allows locking up an interest rate for a specified amount of time.

The key, though, is to achieve a comfortable level of growth and/or income after taxes and after inflation. Consider for a moment the effects of inflation and taxation on a "safe, risk free" vehicle. If the CD guarantees a rate of 6%, a 1099 form will be issued making the owner liable for taxes on the interest earned. This alone can amount to an after-tax decrease of up to 40%, depending on the level of your federal and state income tax. Now subtract the effects of long-term inflation. That pretax 6% rate becomes 4% after taxes, and possibly 0% after subtracting an average inflation factor. If we were to assume 5% inflation, there is an actual loss of 1% per year. This "safe" strategy is a guaranteed method for losing money after taxes and inflation. The only possible benefit to the investor is the certainty of knowing what is going to happen to the investment, as opposed to other investment vehicles without the same level of certainty.

To differentiate rates of return, the financial industry uses the term *real rate of return*. The real rate of return refers to the after-inflation rate of return of any given investment. It is a reminder that you cannot ignore the potential erosion of your capital. Keeping the real rate of return in mind enables you to compare investments on an even playing field.

As Figure 4.2 illustrates, the impact of taxes and inflation can often produce a negative result on the return of taxable investments, especially for certificates of deposits.

Figure 4.2: History of the After-Tax Rate of Return for Certificates of Deposit

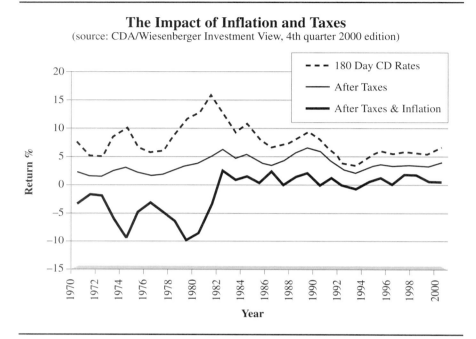

The Impact of Inflation and Taxes

(source: CDA/Wiesenberger Investment View, 4th quarter 2000 edition)

The impact of taxation and inflation can be devastating to long-term financial goals. Before making a decision whether to leave your practice based purely on emotional reasons, investigate the financial implications. What you have accumulated through your retirement plans and personal savings may seem at first glance to be quite substantial. These figures, though, may not hold up to further examination.

Determine the amounts of monthly income that you and your family will need or want. A qualified financial planner can then help you access the feasibility of your financial independence goals. Here assumptions will be made relative to tax rates, inflation, growth of assets, and mortality ages. This feasibility study should provide direction as to your ability to generate income for full retirement as well as determining the financial impact of employment opportunities outside of your practice at lower compensation levels.

Checkup: Financial Independence and Change

As you are making a career change, two other factors will loom large: a current need for financial planning to accomplish your immediate goals and financial independence, with its promise of freedom. Five areas of career change and financial planning affect your long-term goal of financial independence:

Setting Clear Goal

1. Have you set clear goals as you have made your career change?

2. How do your career goals have an impact on short-term and long-term financial goals?

Maximizing Tax Benefits

1. How do you factor taxation into your investment strategy?

2. Have you ever made an investment purely to limit your tax liability? What was the result?

Exercising Discipline

1. Do you make investments regularly and contribute to your retirement plan as defined by law?

2. If you have a self-directed retirement plan, how often do you move investments within the portfolio? What effect have these changes had on the portfolio's overall growth?

Factoring in Inflation

1. What is the current rate of inflation?

2. Do you have any cash accounts, stocks, bonds, or other investments that are yielding less than the current rate of inflation?

Living with Risk

1. How do you tell whether the risk involved in certain investments is appropriate?

2. Have you adjusted the volatility and risk of your investment portfolio as you have aged?

Chapter 5

Legal and Insurance Issues When You Leave a Practice

Steven M Harris

T he method and costs associated with your exit strategy will be determined in large part by the reasons you have chosen to leave your group practice. Obviously, the more your partners and you agree on the strategy, the less time and money will be spent toward its execution.

Leaving a Group Practice

Today's exceedingly competitive environment often finds physicians working for many different practices during a career, and rarely do physicians make a clean break from one practice to another. Most contemplate leaving their current relationship, take affirmative steps to feel out their prospects, and then leave for greener pastures. These changes often result in hard feelings among physicians that are exacerbated by poor planning and insufficient written documentation.

Although natural to discuss a move with current referral sources and patients, such conversations often form the basis for litigation once the physician has officially terminated from the practice and moved to his or her new setting. The prudent physician will reduce or eliminate the risk of litigation by adhering to the following guidelines:

- Do not discuss your move with current patients, referral sources, colleagues, or staff members of the practice.

- Do not divert patient scheduling to your next office location. Accordingly, it is not acceptable to say, "Mrs. Jones, your next appointment is in three weeks. At that time I will be affiliated with a new practice, the address of which is 123 Main Street. Please call my new phone number and schedule your next visit." The amount of risk a physician incurs by engaging in this conversation will depend on several factors including the nature of the restrictive covenants, if any, contained within an employment agreement. Assuming no agreement exists, or if one does exist, no restrictive covenant is contained within it, the physician is not free of risk by engaging in this conduct before terminating employment. Employees, including employed physicians, owe a common-law duty of loyalty to their employers. Therefore, diverting patients to the physician's subsequent relationship will breach the duty of loyalty to the current employer and expose the physician to damages.

- Do not reproduce patient (or referral source) lists that contain mailing addresses, telephone numbers, or the like.

- Read your employment agreement to determine your obligation to afford your employer sufficient notice before termination.

- Read your employment agreement to determine the proper way to give notice (such as first class mail or hand delivery).

- Resign (in writing) your position as an employee of the practice; your role as an officer, if any, of the practice; your position as a member of the board of directors, if any, of the practice; and your role as a trustee, if any, of any qualified retirement plan maintained by the practice.

- Communicate in writing with your present employer in connection with the continuity of care for patients under your control. Make sure the employer responds in writing that your patients will continue to be treated by competent physicians of the practice. This communication will reduce the likelihood of abandonment suits.

- Seek expert legal advice to discuss your intentions *before* making the move. Remember, the conversations that you initiate with counsel are protected by attorney-client privilege. This privilege enables you to instruct your lawyer to keep the discussions confidential. Do not be afraid to "tell all" to your attorney in an effort to reduce your legal exposure when changing practice affiliations.

Get Good Counsel

Get a good lawyer to assist you in navigating these murky waters. How do you find someone qualified? Ask colleagues who have been through similar situations for a referral. Ask the lawyer who handles your real estate matters or your wills and trusts for a referral.

Remember, in many respects law and medicine are similar. If you encounter a specialized problem, seek a lawyer who has that particular training and experience. You would no sooner see a dermatologist for a cardiovascular problem than a divorce lawyer for a partnership dispute.

Further, ask the lawyer to whom you were referred if the firm represents physicians in partnership dissolutions. General business lawyers who have represented partners in commercial disputes are often ill equipped to represent the special needs of a physician involved in a similar situation. Ask how many similar cases the firm has worked on in the previous year. Ask for the names of several current clients of the firm who will entertain a telephone call from you asking about their experiences. Determine whether the "chemistry" between you and your lawyer is good. Remember, your lawyer works for you, and you must control the scope of the representation. Far too often attorneys control the outcomes of partnership disputes, leaving their clients feeling disenfranchised from the process and quite a bit poorer to boot.

Keep Disputes Private

Keeping your partnership conflict outside the gossip of the doctor's lounge will be difficult. Information typically leaks out in a variety of ways, most often by staff members of the practice or the doctors themselves. It is most often advantageous to limit the public disclosure of the conflict. Neither side wins the public relations battle, and often, both sides lose. Try to limit the information that leaks to the hospital administration, medical plans, referral sources, and, most important, to the patients.

If you are practicing within a hospital-based physician group, such as radiology, pathology, emergency medicine, and so on, maintaining the privacy of the dispute is most important. It is not uncommon to learn of situations in which an administrator has elected to bring an entirely new provider group to the hospital rather than attempt to officiate the internal disruptions of the current contract holder.

One of the surest ways to protect the privacy of the facts and circumstances that surround a dispute is to set forth in the partnership agreement that all conflicts must be resolved through binding arbitration. Unlike more traditional judicial forums, arbitration panels will not publish their findings other than to the involved parties. Federal and state courts, on the other hand, make available to the general public all complaints and responses. The court system is also freely accessible to the general public. In higher profile matters of interest to the public, media are often present so that they can get the story firsthand for tomorrow's newspapers and newscasts.

The only way to guarantee access to arbitration is to specify it in writing in the partnership agreement. Even without such a provision, the disputing partners can agree to submit to binding arbitration. The later opportunity only exists if all parties to the dispute are willing to agree to arbitration. When partners are feuding, even the simplest agreements can become difficult. Often, once a dispute arises, one party decides that it is advantageous to resolve the conflict in court, thereby eliminating arbitration.

A typical arbitration clause will contain several promises. First, each party waives the right to bring the dispute in any other forum. If a conflict arises, each party to the dispute designates one qualified, disinterested party willing to act as arbitrator. It may be helpful to define the qualifications of the arbitrators within the agreement. (Perhaps disinterested health-care attorneys or retired judges experienced in these matters will serve the process well.) The two arbitrators jointly select a third, and a panel of three hears the claims and counterclaims of the parties. The panel may render its decision within several days of the completion of the presentations.

One factor to consider when selecting arbitration as the dispute resolution forum is the remedy being sought. Typically, arbitration panels only resolve disputes that involve money. Often, disputes among partners require one party seeking the enforcement of a restrictive covenant. By definition, money damages must be proven to be an inadequate remedy for a party to be successful in enforcing a restrictive covenant. In such situations, it may be appropriate for parties to split the way that they will resolve the dispute: Consider allowing the cost-effective, private arbitration panel to hear all disputes concerning money, while seeking equitable relief in the more traditional court system.

In all cases, consider an agreement that sets forth the prevailing parties' entitlement to recover all expenses associated with the dispute as an element of damages from the nonprevailing party. The thought of financing "the other side's" legal, accounting, and consulting costs in addition to your own—plus the possibility of paying damages to your ex-partner— often acts as a tremendous deterrent to fighting in the first place. Without written language in the agreements assessing such costs to the losing party, each partner will bear his or her own expenses, whether in arbitration or litigation.

Resolve Disputes about Restrictive Covenants

Perhaps the most hotly contested issue in any partnership dispute is the enforceability of a restrictive covenant. As we saw above, these disputes are most often resolved through conventional court proceedings. The emotion and money of the participants flow freely.

Courts recognize the application of restrictive covenants but disfavor their enforceability. Parties may wish to focus their negotiations on compensatory payments other than pinning their hopes on equitable relief. By enabling departing partners to buy out of the restrictions contained within their agreements, the parties may find themselves with an alternative to the uncertain results of seeking an injunction.

Similarly, partnership agreements should contain provisions that limit or eliminate payments to departing partners who choose to violate the terms of a restrictive covenant and compete within the geographic area prohibited within the agreement. Without the benefit of such a provision, the practice may find itself in the untenable position of financing the startup of a new competitor while losing a portion of its patient following to the same party.

Some practices find it beneficial to pay partners more money upon termination in exchange for an agreement not to compete. For example, a partner may receive 150% of his or her accounts receivable if she resigns from the practice and retires or joins a practice outside the geographic area set forth in the agreement. The practice may then withhold all (or a percentage of) these payments in the event the partner competes.

To be effective, the payments owed to the withdrawing partner should begin several months after termination and be paid in installments thereafter. That way, the practice will be sure the former partner has decided not to compete within the first several months immediately after separation, typically the most critical to preserving the goodwill of the practice. The delay in payment also gives the practice an opportunity to seek an injunction against its former colleague while forcing him or her to use personal funds to defend the court action.

In addition to the traditional prohibitions found within restrictive covenants, written agreements should include supporting provisions to preserving practice goodwill, as outlined in the sections that follow.

Observe the Prohibition against Employing Practice Personnel

The withdrawing partner should be prohibited from employing those persons employed (or retained in the case of an independent contractor) by the practice within six months of the partner's withdrawal. Prohibiting "solicitation" for employment of practice personnel will not be a sufficient barrier to a departing partner who can allege that the subject staff member approached him or her about a position with the new practice. Moreover, the 6-month requirement is important to protect the practice from an employee terminating immediately before a withdrawing partner and thus technically not be employed at the instant the partner quits.

Protect Referral Sources

Specialty practices often miss protecting the most important aspect of goodwill by focusing on their patients rather than referral sources. While it is natural for a practice to think of protecting its patient base, prohibiting withdrawing partners from contacting, soliciting, and accepting referrals from sources known to the practice during the partner's tenure is essential. Cutting off an ex-partner from sources of business is an exceptional deterrent to competition.

Know the Effects of Antisolicitation Agreements

Just as it is important to prohibit the solicitation of employees, it is equally important to protect the patients and referral sources from the solicitation of a partner who has withdrawn from the practice. Unfortunately, the word *solicitation* has no exact legal definition. Therefore, courts and arbitration panels across the country are faced with the specific facts and circumstances of each case to determine if a party has violated the antisolicitation clause within the agreement. To avoid uncertainty, define solicitation within the agreement and include direct contact; indirect contact when an agent of a withdrawn partner makes contact on his behalf; announcements in newspapers or periodicals intended to reach your patients and referral sources; and a prohibition against producing zip code mailings within the specific geographic area of the restriction.

Protect Hospital Staff Privileges

The agreement may seek to further protect the practice by requiring a withdrawing partner to resign from the medical staffs of hospitals located within the protected geographic area of the restrictive covenant. This can result in a punitive measure if the medical staff is closed during the period of restriction and the departing physician is unable to gain admission after the covenant period concludes.

Retiring From a Group Practice

Retiring from the practice of medicine is certainly less contentious than leaving your current practice for a competitor across the street. When a physician retires, the event is typically preceded by months or even years of planning. This window enables the practice to plan for a seamless transition of patients and legal responsibilities for all concerned. The agreements between the practice and the physician should address the retirement process as well as the financial obligations each has to the other.

Insurance Issues Involved in Changing Your Practice

When a partner leaves a practice, it is often the objective of both sides to make a clean break. Sometimes, although each party agrees upon such a termination, third parties invoke superior rights that keep ex-partners together (usually through counsel) well beyond their respective desires. These cases arise when, during the relationship, the partners entered obligations jointly and severally. The most common forms of these commitments are leases and bank promissory notes.

Joint and Several Liability

Unknown to many physicians, most loans and leases are structured as joint and several among all partners within the practice. Each party to the loan, lease, or other obligation is responsible for the entire debt. The result of such a provision means that, upon default by the practice, the bank or landlord may collect all amounts due from one partner—even if the partner is now a former partner. Leaving the practice does not affect the rights of third parties to enforce joint and several obligations agreed upon while the partners practiced together.

Often, settlement agreements among the partners state that former partners shall be indemnified against financial exposure in connection with a lease or bank note. The practice and the remaining partners "take over" the obligation for the withdrawing partner. However, there is often little, if any, incentive for the bank or landlord to release any partner to the obligation unless fresh consideration—usually money—is paid for the release. Therefore, even though the remaining partners have "guaranteed" the former partner of no trailing liability, that promise is only as good as their continued creditworthiness. The former partner, if obligated to pay any portion of the liability after the execution of the settlement agreement, has the legal right to seek reimbursement from former partners. However, it is likely that the financial condition of those left behind is not healthy, resulting in a great legal theory but no real remedy.

As part of any termination or settlement agreement, it is essential that all departing partners review every obligation of the practice that may result in joint and several personal liability. Withdrawing partners should approach the lender, landlord, or other creditor to ascertain what actions, if any, will be necessary to secure release from the obligation. That way, the failure of the practice to meet its future financial obligations will not result in an unexpected telephone call or letter from your former bank or landlord demanding payment for a debt unrelated to your current practice.

Covering Your Tail: The Reporting Endorsement Dilemma

Understanding the financial responsibilities between the practice on the one hand and the withdrawing physician-partner on the other has its potentially greatest impact when confronting the purchase of a reporting endorsement—commonly referred to as *tail coverage.* Tail coverage is often necessary when a physician leaves a practice covered by claims-made professional liability insurance. Claims-made coverage will protect a physician for professional negligence as long as a two-part test is met: The claim must have arisen while the physician was practicing medicine on behalf of the practice. In addition, the physician must be placed on notice that the claim is pending while the physician is still engaged on behalf of that practice. If either of these tests is not met, the current claims-made insurance policy will not provide coverage.

The most common failure of the test results when a physician leaves a practice after providing professional services on its behalf without knowledge of a pending claim. If the physician joins another practice insured by a separate company and subsequently learns of a claim resulting from services performed during the previous practice relationship, the physician will fail the claims-made coverage test invoked by the current carrier.

To avoid this break in coverage, physicians have only a few options. The most common (and sometimes the only) option chosen by the physician is the purchase of a reporting endorsement—or tail coverage—that insures the withdrawing physician's professional acts after he or she leaves a practice insured by claims-made coverage.

Unfortunately, the cost of such coverage is often prohibitive, with premium prices well in excess of $100,000 for certain high-risk specialties. A physician who faces the burden of paying for his or her own tail coverage may find it necessary to accept a position with an employer who provides a retroactive date covering professional services from the beginning of the previous practice relationship rather than a position that provides greater satisfaction or better career opportunities. Sometimes, physicians are forced from private practice altogether, finding only hospitals and faculty foundations willing to accept retroactive date coverage as a condition of employment.

Practice Alert: Who Is Responsible for Tail Coverage?

Terminating physicians are smart to focus their attention on a trap often played out in the context of tail coverage. A practice may have the financial responsibility for getting tail coverage on behalf of a terminating physician. In many cases, the physician may be leaving the practice for another within the same state and insured by the same insurance carrier. In those situations, the carrier will maintain seamless insurance coverage for the physician without the need for a tail. However, if the partnership or employment agreement sets forth the affirmative obligation of the practice to purchase a reporting endorsement, the physician is wise to enforce that right. Because tail insurance has the effect of covering all of the prior professional history of the physician, subsequent insurance underwriting will treat that physician as a first-year risk, thereby substantially reducing the cost of future premium payments and perhaps ultimately a second tail policy. This is the case even though the physician may have many years of professional experience.

This result may have profound economic impact on the physician who is charged for professional liability premiums as a personal expense and thus bears 100% of its cost against the production of future income. Moreover, in the event the physician leaves the second practice responsible for his or her own tail coverage, the cost associated with underwriting that risk for one or two years will be dramatically less than for a mature policy.

An example of the financial impact of getting tail coverage on future insurance premiums follows. Suppose a cardiac surgeon practicing in Cook County, Illinois needs to purchase tail coverage after six years in private practice. The cost of such coverage will approximate $170,000. The following year, the insurance underwriters will assess a premium of $20,000 to cover the cost of professional liability for the physician. If this premium seems low, it is. The purchase of the tail in effect insured all prior risk, rendering the cardiologist entering his seventh year of practice, a first year risk with no prior claims exposure. Had the cardiologist not procured tail coverage—or not forced his group to purchase it on his behalf—the seventh year premium would cost the physician $80,000.

For the foregoing reasons, partnership agreements must set forth the responsibility to purchase tail coverage. Often, a physician will earn the right to a percentage (say, 25%) of the tail premium for each year she provides professional services for the practice. In this case, a physician would need to work for the practice for four complete years before the practice bought 100% of the premium associated with the coverage. The physician and practice can also negotiate that tail coverage will be paid by the party responsible for terminating the relationship.

Creating harmony among physicians changing their practice affiliations—whether through retirement, separation, or otherwise—may be a lofty goal. It can, however, be obtained through effective communication coupled with a basic understanding and respect for your former associates. Understanding your rights and setting forth, in writing, the basic principles of your relationship will undoubtedly provide an excellent basis for maximizing the opportunity for peace.

Checkup: Lowering the Risk of Conflict as You Make Your Career Change

The following is a list of actions with potential to cause conflict (and conflicts of interest) with your old practice group. If you cannot check off one or more of the following statements, circle the statement and decide on how you should go about minimizing conflict — and your legal exposure.

❏ I have kept information about my move confidential and have not discussed the change with other staff members.

❏ I have not given information to my patients that may seem as though I were diverting them from the old practice to my new one.

❏ I have not reproduced patient lists or patients' addresses and telephone numbers.

❏ I have read my employment agreement thoroughly and understand all of the clauses.

❏ I have given sufficient notice under the terms of my employment or partnership agreement.

❏ I gave notice in writing.

❏ I have given written instructions on how to maintain continuity of care for my patients.

❏ I understand how my employment contract or partnership agreement requires me to resolve disputes.

❏ I have discussed restrictive covenants in my contract or agreement with a lawyer who specializes in representing physicians.

❏ I have discussed joint and several liability issues with a lawyer who specializes in representing physicians.

❏ I have ascertained who is responsible for "tail coverage" and who will pay for the reporting endorsement.

Chapter 6

Using Resources and Relationships to Ease Your Transition

Peter S Moskowitz, MD

Planning a Successful Transition

Physicians who are contemplating relocating their practice face a challenging series of decisions that may threaten to consume them. Before undertaking such an important career change, it is wise to spend some time reflecting on Frederic M Hudson's Cycle of Renewal model as articulated in his *The Adult Years: Mastering the Art of Self-Renewal* and *LifeLaunch, A Passionate Guide to the Rest of Your Life*[1,2] (see Chapter 1).

Locating Yourself in the Renewal Cycle

The first order of business for physicians contemplating change is to identify which of the four stages of the career cycle they are in: Phase 1 (Go for It), Phase 2 (Doldrums), Phase 3 (Cocooning), or Phase 4 (Exploring). This can best be done by deciding which of the markers and identifiers of each respective stage most closely describe their current attitudes and feelings (see Figure 1-1 in Chapter 1, "Psychological Preparation for Change"). Most often, they will find themselves in Phase 2; however, planning to relocate or modify clinical practice is possible from within any of the four career stages, depending on the specific circumstances of the situation.

Physicians in Phase 2 can best manage their transition by first determining what has worked well in the current setting and then identifying what has not worked well. Some people find it useful to record the details in a personal journal for reflection and future planning. Eventually, a decision must be made to let go of some or all of the facets of the current practice or practice group that have not worked effectively and to move on. People in Phase 2 can most successfully recycle their career back into Phase 1 either through a minitransition or by making a full career transition.

The Minitransition

A minitransition involves making some relatively minor career change(s) intended to create new challenge and fulfillment and to lead people back into Phase 1 of the career cycle. Typically, the minitransition will take up to six months and usually will not involve a change in clinical focus or specialization. For some, this career reengineering may include a geographic change in practice, a change in practice group within the same geographic location, or both. For others, it may mean a change from an academic setting to a private practice setting or vice versa. For still others, it may mean learning a new clinical skill within the confines of their own field of specialization, or taking coursework to enhance or begin responsibilities in medical staff management.

For example, an internist may obtain training to perform fiberoptic colonoscopy; a general surgeon may obtain training in laparoscopic surgery; or a manager may take a course in mediation and conflict resolution. The end result of such minor clinical reengineering is that the physician obtains a new skill set that serves to enhance self-esteem and update clinical skills and knowledge, thereby enabling him or her to make a new contribution to his or her practice or group.

Simply relocating one's practice to a new location or finding a new medical group structure will usually generate sufficient new challenges to reinvigorate most physicians. This effort typically recreates a sense of excitement and fulfillment for clinical practice, and the renewed physician reenters Phase 1 of the cycle.

Given a choice between making a minitransition and making a full major transition, most physicians will choose the minitransition. It takes less time and effort, often does not involve a relocation of one's primary residence, and creates relatively minor upheavals in cash flow and family life if planned thoughtfully. It is quite possible to make a series of mini-transitions over the time course of a medical career as the need arises, to recreate passion and enthusiasm at work and avoid boredom. For mid-career physicians aged fifty and over, the minitransition is an excellent strategy for escaping the doldrums. One or two minitransitions may be all that is necessary to sustain themselves until they no longer have the interest, desire, or financial need to continue clinical practice.

The minitransition creates a dilemma, however, for the 30- to 40-year old or younger physician in the doldrums. The reason for the dilemma is that the duration of Phase 1 following a minitransition is somewhat shorter than the original Phase 1, or the Phase 1 following a full life transition. Accordingly, as each successive minitransition is of shorter and shorter duration, eventually an individual may find himself or herself spinning in a tight circle within the cycle, having exhausted ideas for more minitransitions and screwing themselves into the ground, to use a visual analogy. At that point of career desperation, minitransitions will work no longer. The only remaining choice is a major transition.

The Major Transition

A major transition is the process by which one moves around the periphery of the career cycle from Phase 2 (Doldrums) into Phase 3 (Cocooning), eventually reaching Phase 4 (Exploring), and then finally back to Phase 1 (Go for It). It is a process that takes time. The duration of a typical major professional career transition averages three years but often lasts longer. The lives and careers of physicians are complex; changes take a great deal of time and planning.

The full life transition begins with movement into Phase 3. For some physicians this movement occurs without their free will when their position in a medical organization is downsized, when they are fired, or when they lose their license to practice. It is often a time of great emotional turmoil and discomfort. For a smaller group of more fortunate physicians, a voluntary decision is made to make a major career and life change, and they have the time and resources to allow this to happen naturally.

The cocooning process is one of quiet self-reflection, a time of self-rediscovery. It is often, but not necessarily, a time away from clinical medicine. It may take the form of a sabbatical or extended vacation time. Some practices permit a leave of absence without pay. Physicians may elect to slow down by taking an extra day off each week, use locum tenems coverage to take more time off or less night or weekend call, or reduce the size of their patient load. The extra time gained from these valuable strategies can be used by the resourceful physician to cocoon. Physicians who have lost their jobs have the opportunity to cocoon full-time for as long as they can manage financially.

Phase 3 is a time to explore your values, purpose, and passions. For most busy professionals, these important aspects of self often have not been explored consciously since early adulthood or even longer. Often the values, sense of purpose, and passions of early adult life have been quietly shed or have evolved in unexpected ways as a consequence of our own unique life experience. Yet daily life and career decisions are still being made on the basis of this outdated sense of self. Many discover during cocooning that those important aspects of self were in fact programmed within us as children or early adults by others.

Perhaps they were well-wishing parents, relatives, spouses, teachers, or mentors. The important thing is that we come to realize in Phase 3 that those values are no longer ours. To move forward and discover a new destiny for ourselves, we must first clarify and become grounded in our current, authentic values, purpose, and passions. We get a chance to rediscover our true identity.

The internal work that must be done is hard to do alone. It is a task that challenges most physicians at their deepest levels. They must accept, at least to themselves, that they do not have all the answers, and they must learn to ask for professional help to obtain those answers. What's more, they must accept their own vulnerability during the process. Excellent support sources to assist with this cocooning work include psychotherapists, psychologists, career/life coaches, career counselors, wise physician colleagues, and spiritual counselors. In Phase 3, physicians who spend time alone learn techniques to listen within and to trust the voice that they hear, often for the first time in their lives.

Having a quiet cocoon within which to feel safe, secure, and listen is important. It provides a shelter for the physician to plan and undergo an internal transformation, just as the cocoon does for the caterpillar.

Practice Alert: Some Techniques to Spark Transition

Reading self-help literature—especially titles about careers and work—may prove productive as you make a transition. Because physicians tend to be highly educated and verbal, taking tests that reveal personality features, skills, career paths, and interests may be useful, too. These tests, often found in books on career paths, can be handy because they give you a chance to see your ideas on paper and to make an inventory of your accomplishments, character traits, and desires. Spending time alone is helpful because it frees you to think deeply and without interruptions. Finally, keeping a journal, praying, or meditating sometimes start the flow of new ideas.

Assessing Transition Resources

During the early stages of transition planning, whether for a minitransition or a major transition, the physician must give appropriate time and thought to the assessment of resources available for support during transition. Such resources include but are not limited to time, money, professional help, and family and external support.

Time

Above all else, transitions take time, but time is often the physician's most scarce resource. Careful thought must be given to time management and how the physician can use time to support his or her values about career or life change. This work will best be done in conjunction with a career/life coach, career counselor, or therapist. The physician will need to make a conscious effort to take something off the "plate" to make room for transition planning. Special leaves, sabbaticals, and extra vacation can be used by physicians for this purpose. In the absence of any of these time resources, transitions can be effectively planned by consistently carving out time during days off or weekends, or both.

Money

The immediate consequence of reduced clinical presence or leaves of absence is a reduction in income. There is no getting around that truth. Coupled with falling practice income and reimbursement associated with managed care, money issues often become the deal-breaker in transition planning. Accordingly, strict budgeting, detailed cash-flow and income projections, and good tax planning must become mainstays of transition planning. These issues are always hard to confront and can produce intense anxiety both for the physician and the spouse or partner. Professional help from a fee-only financial planner or CPA is often necessary to reassure all the players that financial disaster will not be the unintended outcome. Assessing financial resources and making use of financial planning professionals is equally important for the physician who enters transition owing to loss of job or license.

Professional Help

Although the battle cry of the physician is, "I can handle this myself", adequate transition planning should include the help of both career and mental health professionals. Transition planning is inherently stressful; confronting the need for change is difficult. The typical physician is socially isolated with few intimate personal friendships and few friends outside the immediate sphere of health care. The result of all of these factors is that physicians get little objective feedback from others about their own social and personal choices and lifestyle. Similarly, they typically do not have sources of emotional support beyond their spouses or partners to fall back on in times of personal need. Left to their own devices and thought patterns, physicians will tend to avoid or procrastinate, or both, rather than take steps toward change. Many will become mired in fear resulting from their own need for perfection.

Career counselors and career coaches can be extremely helpful to the physician in planning a career change. They are professionally trained to encounter and work with the internal resistance and fears of clients undergoing career transition. Such professionals help can clarify the client's purpose in seeking change and elicit the professional values that support client satisfaction. In this way, they help link inner values with outer work. They can also assist in developing a vision for the future and establishing a purposeful plan to actualize that career vision. When necessary, they can provide access to standardized career assessment tools to clarify a client's interests, motivated skills, marketable skills, and personality profile. Perhaps most importantly, they provide the physician with the care, support, and accountability they need to help guarantee that intended actions and changes do take place.

Mental health professionals also may play an important role in supporting the physician in transition. Before the work to envision, plan for, and instigate a job change can start, underlying emotional resistance and major depression may have to be dealt with first. Unfortunately, the physician often finds it difficult to ask for help from a mental health professional until his or her life is in chaos. He or she often is unaware of the emotional component; the spouse or a co-worker may be the first to notice. Chronic stress and dissatisfaction at work eventually lead to changes in behavior and attitude, including increased irritability and loss of empathy. Conflicts often increase with co-workers, who may view the physician as easily angered, uncooperative, and distractible. Eventually the physician may become withdrawn and uncaring, becoming less involved in practice issues and concerns.

At home the disgruntled physician retreats from family life and fun, often to get lost in television, or other distractions. Sleep may become disrupted. The physician may lose interest in hobbies and love making. Eventually, physical health begins to deteriorate. Headaches, hypertension, inappropriate weight gain or loss, and symptoms of gastrointestinal disorders or coronary artery disease may develop. These emotional and physical signs of stress and burnout must be addressed before a full health crisis ensues.

Counseling with a mental health care professional is often necessary to stabilize the life of a physician in transition or burnout. A stable, relatively calm life setting is necessary for the physician to move forward with difficult decisions to modify his or her work or home environment to achieve greater personal and professional satisfaction. Most physicians facing a major career or job transition benefit from short-term psychotherapy to clarify and work through the strong feelings that invariably arise. Additionally, psychotherapy is always indicated with or without psychopharmacologic intervention when major depression or other mental disorders interfere with normal function.

Family Support

Often, a physician's spouse is his or her best friend as well. The spouse therefore naturally becomes the principal source of emotional support for the physician undergoing career transition. Both partners should discuss plans for job change and anticipate the gains and losses that may ensue from such a decision. They should honestly appraise how such a career change could be used to better meet professional, personal, and family and relationship priorities.

Furthermore, decisions that materially alter the physician's practice usually have ramifications in other parts of their lives and marriage; these demand mutual discussion and agreement. For all of these reasons, the spouse of a transitioning physician can expect turbulent times. He or she may be in the awkward position of wanting to be supportive through the stressful changes, while also ensuring that his or her own needs are figured into the decision-making process. Both people's needs are important and need to be honored. Sometimes, however, the needs of the physician appear to be in direct conflict with those of the spouse. Such conflicts between physician and spouse during transition commonly arise over the potential for income and lifestyle changes brought on by a job transition. For example, a physician may envision a new job involving a reduction in the intensity of his or her current practice effort, such as a part-time arrangement. Although the physician is willing to accept the consequence of lower professional income, the spouse may view this as an abrogation of the physician's often unspoken "contract" to continue to provide for the spouse and children according to their existing lifestyle. In such cases, consultation with a counselor or financial planner, or both, may be necessary to reach an appropriate, mutually agreeable compromise. Such a compromise must respect previous financial goals established by the couple, or lead to a renegotiation of those goals.

Although it would be inappropriate to expect a physician's children to offer emotional support during transition, it is important to discuss a new job with children once a decision to change has been made. Children will have a natural curiosity about what is going to happen and whether there will be an impact on their lives. They deserve to know the basics without flooding them with information. It is empowering for children to realize that parents may have problems and issues at work that can be managed successfully through dialogue and planning. When parents are resilient and creative through difficult times, including job transition, children learn that they, too, can be resilient and creative with regard to their own problems.

External Support

It is important for the physician facing job transition to stay connected to friends and colleagues and to use them as sources of support as necessary. Such contact keeps the physician in contact with objective thinking and a fresh perspective about things. Human contact is also a source of stress relief and a buffer against the strain of impending change. Shared experiences around the topics that come up during transition planning offer the physician who is contemplating change some comfort and useful information.

Recruit the Support of Key Relationships

In addition to recruiting the support of spouse, significant others, family, and friends, certain key relationships can make career transition a smoother experience. If you are considering making a professional change, having a close working relationship with a financial planner who is familiar with your financial plan is to your advantage. Make contact early in the decision-making process and let the planner provide assistance, suggestions, cash flow projections for the new practice opportunity, projections for any refinancing of debt being considered, and an assessment of the impact of the new practice opportunity on your existing retirement plan and investment plan for educating children. In addition, a professional career coach or career counselor may provide resources and support if you are unsure of the best way to proceed or just what kind of change would be most suitable.

Sources for emotional support may include a psychotherapist, counselor, spiritual advisor, mentor, colleague, or friend. In some medical communities there are existing physician support groups that meet regularly to discuss practice and life issues. At the beginning of a career transition, it is useful to make contact with such resources and seek their understanding and support. This is particularly important if you have not maintained a support system in your personal life.

Create a Support Network Before You Leave

Using all of the key relationship and resources mentioned above, plan ahead for an impending job transition before it occurs. This means considering what might possibly go wrong, get delayed, or cost more than planned. Ask yourself: What may be the emotional burdens to pay? How may the transition adversely affect other family members? How can I best anticipate these problems and deal with them as a professional, as a spouse, and as a parent? Consider these questions and discuss them with appropriate members of your support network in advance. Thinking through the issues and creating strategies in advance makes the actual transition smoother and less anxiety provoking.

If the transition involves a major relocation of the practice and/or the principal residence, the physician would do well to consider before the move how best to provide the key services and support in the new location as well. While some or all key relationships may be able to be maintained by telecommunications, the interpersonal sources of support are difficult to sustain by long distance. New resources may need to be identified in the new community prior to the move to facilitate the transition while it occurs.

Plan Your Goodbye: Rituals and Ceremonies

All new beginnings are accompanied by an ending. We often celebrate the new beginnings and forget to honor and celebrate the endings also. By honoring the endings, we are able to acknowledge and show appropriate gratitude for the good times, happy experiences, and the positive working relationships that have characterized a work environment. It also gives co-workers an opportunity to thank the departing colleague for all that colleague has contributed to the enterprise over time. These ceremonies serve a useful purpose: to enable the departing individuals to let go more easily of each other and take on the new.

If we fail to celebrate endings, not only do we lose the opportunity to acknowledge the positive, but we may also be left with unresolved negative emotions or resentments about former employers, working partners, or past events. Those resentments may haunt us and our memories for years after we leave. They may also significantly interfere with healthy adjustments to new work settings. Accordingly, it is wise to plan an appropriate ending ceremony or ritual to commemorate this end of a phase of their working life.

Such a celebration can take many forms; there is no formula for success other than to make it fun. It can be a small, intimate dinner party for your physician colleagues, or a large, noisy bash for the entire staff. It can be held at the workplace during the day, or offsite after work. Providing an opportunity to say a few words to those remaining behind is always appropriate and the converse is also true. Try to keep it fun and light. Even if there are resentments and regrets, such celebrations are not the appropriate time or place to express them.

Sustaining Your Balance

The process of leaving one practice setting to establish a new one requires patience, finesse, courage, high energy, and good interpersonal and stress management skills. Walking the tightrope between old and new requires a good sense of balance—balance in the manner in which you end existing working relationships with patients and staff, and balance in the way you manage your time, the demands of the new practice situation, and the way you take care of your own needs during the transition.

Maintain Appropriate Boundaries

Once a physician has made a decision to leave a practice setting, one of the most difficult tasks of getting out gracefully is maintaining good boundaries between the old practice setting, and the new one. As soon as the terms of a new job are negotiated and finalized, there is a flourish of activity and communications, including the processing of legal documents both for the new practice as well as with for the old one. Both sides will expect you to respond to requests to provide information quickly; and both parties will also expect you to keep the terms of employment private. Although it is always important to be honest, it is best to keep private any information of a personal or business nature about either practice.

When there have been resentments or a history of prior difficulties, the departing physician may be tempted to sabotage the old practice through inappropriate disclosure of patient information, business practices, or personal information about other physicians. Avoid the temptation. Do not burn your bridges behind you; leave the practice on good terms.

Preserve Professional Relationships

As discussed above, it is always to your advantage to sustain good relationships with former partners, associates, and institutions. One never knows when there will be a need to cooperate with former associates or institutions in the management of patients, to forge new cooperative business ventures, to request special treatment for new patients, or even to seek letters of personal reference for new professional opportunities. For all of these reasons, it makes good sense to preserve good will whenever possible. During the transition, this is best done by maintaining honest and open communication with outgoing practice associates, accepting more than your share of patient care and business responsibilities, and maintaining a pleasant and cooperative attitude at all times. Don't give anyone an excuse to give you a bad reputation.

Avoid Creating Feelings of Abandonment

Whenever physicians leave a practice, certain patients and staff may feel abandoned. Even in the best of circumstances, and with more than adequate notice to patients, colleagues, and staff, there frequently is unhappiness with the departing physician. If you are in transition, take precautions to provide adequate notice and suggest alternative sources of care to each patient. Several months' advance notice is a minimum. It is wise to schedule an open meeting with your patients in which you can announce your new plans, discuss suitable alternatives for the continuity of their medical care, and answer their questions.

Be aware that co-workers, including non-physician staff and fellow physicians, may harbor similar feelings of abandonment. Those feelings may not be expressed openly but may get acted out by way of sarcasm—or through emotional or physical distancing.

Physician associates and the medical organizations for which you and they work deserve to get as much advance notice of your intention to leave as is reasonably possible and legally mandated by your employment agreement. Be sure to review your employment agreement before giving notice.

Maintain Your Usual Work Schedule

As you prepare to move to a new job, you might be tempted to reduce your work schedule. There will be innumerable details to attend to. Be aware that this very circumstance may feed into the resentment or jealousy, or both, that some of your associates and staff may be experiencing around your decision to leave. When you decrease your work hours, it may cause your about-to-become former associates to work longer hours to cover the shortfall in clinical coverage. Coming on the heels of other potential resentments, there is the potential for much ill will. An additional reason for maintaining your usual schedule is that many of your patients will want to see you during the last weeks you are with your current practice to say their good-byes and to seek answers to last-minute questions before they switch to another physician.

In short, you can best avoid problems by maintaining a full work schedule right up until the last day on the job. It provides less fodder for complaints by patients and co-workers.

Self Care During Transition

Your level of stress will increase significantly during your practice transition. For all of the reasons provided above, you will be pulled in every direction. You can anticipate the need to plan and communicate with managers and administrators at the new job. At the same time you will be closing up your responsibilities at your current practice. You may well be scouting the real estate market for a new home closer to your new practice. Current patients and co-workers will want to communicate with you on a variety of topics. Your family will be making plans requiring your input in anticipation of the new job. Somewhere in this morass of activity you must find the time to remain centered and take good care of yourself.

The mainstay of your self-care program should be a basic daily commitment to the six domains of life balance: physical balance, emotional balance, spiritual balance, relationship balance, community balance, and work and career balance. Achieving balance requires attention to all these domains.

However, balance is rarely present in the lives of busy physicians. Many of us do not have a clear vision of what balance is or how to acquire it. Most of us have lived our entire adult lives out of balance, believing that imbalance is the price of following a calling to medicine. To the extent to which we succeed in attaining balance, we will tap into the most powerful source of insulation against stress and professional burnout.

Physical Balance *Physical balance* refers to wellness, body conditioning, strength, endurance, flexibility, and resistance to disease. People who are physically balanced are in good physical health and have abundant energy. You can maintain good physicial balance during transition by instituting and maintaining a physician-directed wellness program. Begin by getting an annual general physical checkup from your own physician. You can tap into previous sports passions and physical skills to sustain and energize your wellness program. You can explore hidden desires and take new physical risks. Both are challenges for personal growth.

Emotional Balance *Emotional balance* refers to a state of calmness and resilience. People who are emotionally balanced can accept positive and negative input without excessive mood swings. They are aware of their feelings, which they accept and manage. You can maintain good emotional balance during transition by developing a daily program for self-awareness through meditation, prayer, journal writing, or dream analysis. Some people simply give themselves some quiet time alone regularly. Consider undergoing mindfulness training to stay focused in the current moment, enabling you to let go of yesterday and not worry about tomorrow. You can also lean on your support network, mentioned earlier in this section, to discuss your successes and frustrations.

Spiritual Balance *Spiritual balance* refers to a state of connectedness to self, community, and a power beyond oneself. People who are spiritually balanced feel as if they belong to a greater whole. They are hopeful rather than fearful. You can attain spiritual balance during job transition by maintaining your own spiritual program on a daily basis. If you need support or advice, seek a spiritual advisor who can help sustain and nurture your spiritual practice and knowledge. Begin by devoting one hour per week to your spiritual practice of choice. Learn to listen to and act upon your own inner voice and intuition. Learn to have spontaneous fun; your own or others' children will be good guides. Accept that fear and emotional pain are teachers and a part of life.

Relationship Balance *Relationship balance* refers to a state in which people are able to both give and receive. They feel connected to others and are able to state their needs, wants, and sense of reality without fear of being judged adversely. To develop better relationship balance, you must first develop a relationship with *yourself* through a self-awareness program, through spiritual practice, and through time spent alone. Set life goals yearly and reassess them semiannually, with feedback from others in your support network. Assess all major relationships annually, revising roles if appropriate. Are you giving in proportion with what you receive? Practice good listening skills when conversing with others.

Community Balance *Community balance* refers to having a relationship with a community of people. Giving to that community is balanced by what one receives back from it. This exchange generates energy, gratitude, and selflessness. To develop better community balance, you might adopt a community to join, preferably outside the realm of medicine, and schedule time for weekly involvement. Possible communities include hobby-related, sports-related, or spiritual groups. Volunteer some of your time for special projects that have meaning to you and that offer leadership. Take a risk by sharing your thoughts, feelings, successes, and failures with others in the community. Use the community to support you.

Work Balance *Work balance* refers to an elusive sense of giving to one's occupation or career enough to be valued as a worker, without concurrently losing one's sense of self or individual values. Attaining work balance is a particularly difficult challenge for most of us who have been trained and who work within a workaholic system. To move toward better work balance, recognize that career rewards are no longer linear in relation to effort. Develop financial goals and integrate them with your values, using a certified financial planner if necessary. This process will help to clarify long-term needs for capital and permit rational assessment of what level of income is needed to meet the family's desired lifestyle. In turn, this will help to determine the amount and duration of time you need to devote to clinical practice to obtain your desired goals. Finally, remember that satisfaction in life must come from sources beyond your role as a physician and can be enhanced by developing and pursuing interests beyond medicine.

As balance and happiness develop, you may increasingly value your time alone. You may discover that balance often results in wanting what you already have or in changing aspects of your life that are already under your control. Maintaining balance also requires that you assess your personal values and integrate them into your daily life. Achieving balance is difficult work for even the most committed physician. Living in balance requires a paradigm shift for which physicians are generally unprepared; nor can they sustain the shift by themselves. Success requires a thorough education, an unwavering commitment to change, and a strong support network.

What to Expect

A change in practice environment often brings a breath of fresh air to a physician's professional life. If done with appropriate thought and life planning, moving to a new practice environment can better support your values and purpose and restore professional resilience and self-esteem. In the process, some compromises and sacrifices may be inevitable. Following are some general principles that may be useful as you embark on this journey:

- Focus on what you can change

- Don't run away—instead, run toward what you want

- Make changes in steps or phases—break the inertia

- Continuously scout opportunities

- Don't make medicine your only source of identity

- Develop and use your network and support system

- Face and address your personal pitfalls to success
- Expect unsettling and exciting times

Self-Test: Sustaining Your Balance

As you make your transition, you will have to be nimble to move with grace from your former practice to the new practice or opportunity. Two areas should stay high up on your planning list: maintaining good relations with others and taking care of yourself.

1. To maintain appropriate relationships with your soon-to-be-former colleagues, have you minimized any disputes and kept confidences?

2. To maintain appropriate relationships with subordinates, have you kept information about disputes to yourself and avoided making any promises of future employment?

3. Have you maintained good will in your working relationships—and have you tried to repair any relationships that have become strained by your departure?

4. Have you been sensitive to signals by staff members of feelings of abandonment?

5. What have you done to make sure that your patients do not feel abandoned or neglected? (Patient care obviously requires a great deal of attention, and you may want to keep track in writing of your communications, meetings, and recommendations.)

6. Did you give sufficient notice in writing to the members of the practice? If your partners have indicated that you did not, what have you done to repair the situation?

7. Are you maintaining your regular work schedule? If you cannot, have you kept all affect parties informed of changes in your work schedule? Have you kept disruptions and changes to a minimum?

8. How have you handled your closest personal relationships during your transition? Have you explained your plans and actions fully? Have you relied on others for objectivity, support, and "blowing off steam"?

9. Have you taken care of your physical needs during the transition? Have you maintained physical activity? Have you cared for your body by sleeping more or getting a physical, a massage, or even a new haircut?

References

1. Hudson FM. *The Adult Years: Mastering the Art of Self-Renewal.* San Francisco, Calif: Jossey Bass; 1990, revised 1999.

2. Hudson FM, McLean P. *LifeLaunch, A Passionate Guide to the Rest of Your Life.* Santa Barbara, Calif: The Hudson Press; 1995, revised 2000.

Renewal

Where We Are

In Part I you assessed your situation. In Part II you decided on a course of action, focusing in particular on the financial and legal components of making a major career change.

Where We Are Headed

In Part III you will explore the opportunities that will arise as you put your decision into effect. Chapters 7, 8, and 9 describe how to set up the legal organization of your new practice, with information on the different forms of doing business, real estate issues, and the budget process. You will also explore how to set up the finances of your new practice, including investment planning and securing retirement plans for your employees.

Chapter 7

Starting Over: Making the Right Legal Decisions

Steven M Harris

T he decision to leave your practice has been made. If you have chosen to continue practice, many new challenges await. Making informed choices is more difficult than ever; the issues are complicated and plentiful. Attack this process with vigor and excitement. Learn from astute advisors. Listen to colleagues who have experienced similar career changes. Don't be afraid to ask questions. Most important, make decisions only after you have exhausted all sources of knowledge.

Forms of Doing Business

One of the first decisions facing the new practitioner is the choice of legal form of doing business. Not that long ago, medical providers who practiced alone did so as a sole proprietor while physicians practicing together did so in partnerships. Today, many choices are available, each of which has different legal and tax characteristics.

Sole Proprietor

Many physicians practicing alone remain committed to the sole proprietorship. A *sole proprietor,* though, is not a separate legal entity and offers no protection from liability. The appeal is simplicity, at least until the sole proprietor elects to engage in succession planning for the practice. It is usually not practical for the sole proprietor to offer an associate the opportunity to acquire an equity interest in the practice over a period of time while maintaining the sole proprietorship form of ownership. Table 7.1 outlines the advantages and disadvantages of a sole proprietorship to consider.

Table 7.1: Important Characteristics of a Sole Proprietorship

Advantages	Disadvantages
Simplicity	No creditor protection
Lower costs	Awkward for succession planning

Partnership

Seemingly straightforward, partnership nonetheless presents physicians with potential landmines that are often difficult to avoid. A *partnership* requires two or more "persons" owning an equity interest in an entity that is engaged in a profit-making enterprise. *Persons* does not necessarily mean actual people. Accordingly, many partnerships are formed between corporations, trusts, joint ventures, and other entities created under law. Be wary of operating a medical practice as a general partnership unless the partners are entities that limit or reduce personal liability to the physicians. For example, medical practices are often structured as a partnership of professional corporations wherein each physician maintains exclusive ownership in a corporation. This structure is depicted in Figure 7.1.

There are several advantages of this structure. Perhaps the most significant enables each physician to operate within the framework of a general partnership yet insulate personal liability from claims and obligations apart from the clinical practice of medicine. Operating within a professional corporation will not shield a physician from personal liability in connection with professional negligence, however. In those cases, adequate malpractice insurance and engaging in asset protection planning is essential.

Figure 7.1: A Partnership of Professional Corporations

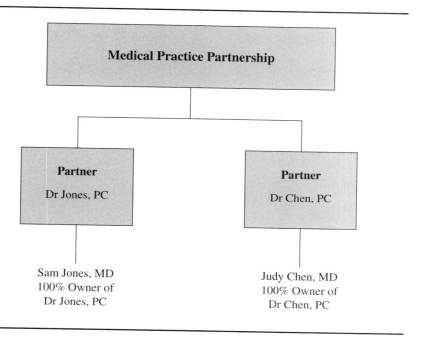

Without the insulation of the professional corporation, each physician would be personally responsible for all claims brought against the partnership and each partner in connection with the business of the entity. Moreover, operating as a partnership of corporations affords physicians great flexibility in compensation and succession planning. Today, however, new entities like the limited liability company and limited liability partnership have found their way into the structure and design of medical practices. Table 7.2 outlines the advantages and disadvantages of a partnership.

Table 7.2: Important Characteristics of Partnerships

Advantages	Disadvantages
Flexibility	Additional tax filings
Useful in succession	Increased personal exposure

Practice Alert: What Does Partnership Mean?

Becoming a partner or joining a partnership raises more questions than it answers. Don't assume that becoming a partner (or co-shareholder in a medical corporation) entitles you to an equal vote in governance issues or compensation equal to your partners in the practice. Nothing could be further from the truth. A specific definition of what the title *partner* means doesn't exist unless it is set forth in an agreement between the parties. Some risk-tolerant partners operate without a written agreement, which exposes them to unintended and potentially catastrophic results in the event of a dispute and dissolution of the practice. Be sure to set down your understandings in a well-crafted document.

Professional Corporations

Today, most group medical practices use the corporation as the entity of choice. The formalities of a professional corporation are similar to business corporations with specific additional regulations that set forth that shareholders and directors of the entity must be licensed physicians. Each state has its own rules, but most follow the legislative intent of precluding "businesspeople" from owning or controlling the direction of medical care. This historical intent has been eroded with the influx of practice management companies assuming more direction over the rendering of medical services through contractual relationships with group practices. States, however, have been unwilling to allow non-physicians to own stock in such practices. Table 7.3 outlines some of the advantages and disadvantages of professional corporations.

Table 7.3: Advantages and Disadvantages of
                Professional Corporations

Advantages	Disadvantages
Increased protection	Compliance with state law
Practical tax planning opportunities	Additional accounting and tax filings

Real Estate Issues

Whether you are going on your own or joining an existing practice, it is imperative that you have a basic understanding of the real estate considerations with respect to the practice. In most cases, those issues will involve a lease for the practice premises. Leases are not created equally. Great care must be taken to identify the issues specific to the practice of medicine.

Use of the Premises

Local law or ordinance will determine if zoning permits the establishment of the practice in your chosen location. If current zoning regulations do not allow such use, be sure to seek counsel immediately to determine the likelihood of obtaining a variance and the time commitment involved in navigating your request through the process. The best-laid plans may be derailed because your inability to quickly obtain approval for the intended use.

When investigating legal and real estate requirements, confirm that the specific specialty practice that you intend to pursue will be allowed by the landlord. For example, the owner may be concerned about the effect your practice will have on other tenants in the building. (You may be more likely to gain approval for an internal medicine practice than an abortion clinic or similar controversial use.) Parking requirements should conform with local ordinance and should also be agreed upon by the landlord.

In addition, rental space is quoted by cost per square foot. Multiplying such cost by the amount of leased space will result in yearly base rental payment obligations to the landlord. Be careful to inquire whether the space is leased on a "net" or "gross" basis. If the space is leased on a net basis, a certain percentage of costs inherent in operating are passed along to each tenant based on its percentage use of the building. Such costs include real estate taxes, insurance, and common area maintenance. It is not uncommon for these costs to approximate the base rent, thereby substantially increasing the initial quote by the landlord.

Cost Allocation

Your practice needs may require substantial modifications to the office space. Usually a landlord will offer a certain dollar amount per square foot leased by a tenant. Always demand the right to independently measure the space offered for lease. Do not simply take on faith that the landlord's quote is accurate.

If your space is measured as 5,000 square feet and the landlord offers a $25-per-square-foot building allowance, you may expect to receive $125,000 from the landlord toward the building of your practice. The allowance must be used to improve the physical premises rather than, for example, to acquire medical equipment or fund working capital.

The allowance is usually part of the financial terms of the lease. If you have no need for an allowance, your rental payments will be less expensive. Be mindful that owners of real estate are likely to build in an interest rate on the allowance "loaned" to your practice. It is therefore always prudent to analyze the cost of the funds from the landlord and compare it to a conventional lender's terms.

Besides the tenant allowance provided by the landlord, the practice itself will also typically contribute money to the buildout of your practice space. In such cases be sure to establish an escrow account at a local title insurance company. The escrow account will serve the purpose of approving invoices and waivers of lien from the various trades that render services in connection with the project. Failure to properly review waivers may result in paying twice for the same services.

Finally, be sure to request a nondisturbance agreement from the mortgage lender of the real estate. The request should be made through the owner of the real estate. A *nondisturbance agreement* sets forth the tenant's right to the premises even though the owner is in default under the note and mortgage that secures the property. Without such an understanding, you may be a tenant with no remedy if the landlord of the property fails to meet its financial obligations to the bank.

Options to Renew

The more expensive the capital expenditure made by the practice, the longer it will typically need to remain in the leased premises to recover its investment. Securing an option to renew the lease after its base period affords the practice an advantage it should not miss. The option will enable the practice to decide at some time in the future whether the location and lease terms remain favorable. Be certain to identify when the option must be exercised. Missed dates often set the stage for expensive disputes.

Lease Cancellations

If you practice alone or in a small-group setting, negotiate the cancellation (at the option of the practice if you have partners) of the lease in the event of your death or permanent disability. Without such a clause, your estate may remain liable for the financial obligations under the lease. Similarly, without such a provision, your disability does not offer an excuse from paying rent throughout the remainder of the term, even though you may not be able to practice medicine.

The Budget Process

Medical practices sometimes fail for the same reasons start-up manufacturing companies do. The main reason often is lack of initial capitalization. Establishing a relationship with a qualified health-care lender is essential.

Like the medical profession, banks (or departments within banks) often specialize. In the case of banks, the specialization is often by industry. It is not uncommon for two banks independent of one another to reach dramatically different conclusions with respect to a request from a medical practice to borrow funds. Those banks in the business of lending to health-care providers and thus comfortable with so-called cash flow lending will underwrite a loan request much differently from a bank looking for capital or inventory as collateral. Asking appropriate questions at the introductory stage of the relationship will save you weeks of delay when time is a critical commodity.

Practice Alert: Questions for Potential Lender

Ask potential lenders relevant questions such as:

1. Do they have experience lending to medical practices?
2. How long may you expect to wait to receive a commitment?
3. Do they require personal guarantees?
4. What other services can you expect to receive from the lender, such as cash management?

How much money you need will, of course, vary from practice to practice. Most start-up practices, however, understand that although medical services may be provided as of the first day the practice opens, collections may lag ninety days or longer. Therefore, when budgeting your liquidity requirements, be sure to include several months of working capital, assuming the practice does not start to collect revenue until the fourth month.

When preparing a request for financing, allow at least three months working capital even though you may be counting on payments from your prior practice affiliation in the form of deferred compensation. It is likely that you are entitled to payments from your prior practice. While you may have a legal right to receive such payments—and therefore understandably rely upon receiving your money—often departing physicians are disappointed to learn that the practice has elected not to make such payments. The practice (which is already upset that you left) may take the position that a breach of contract has occurred. This theory is usually grounded in the restrictive covenant provisions of the partnership agreement. Even if your claim is successful, the delay in its adjudication will create the need to draw on the resources of your financing commitment. On the other hand, if you are fortunate to receive your payments on schedule, seeking access to further funds through a line of credit will cost you nothing. Banks do not charge interest on such credit lines unless and until they are drawn upon.

Although each practice situation may be remarkably different, an example of the start-up costs associated with the establishment of one internal medicine practice with three physicians is shown in Table 7.4.*

Practice Alert: Sketch Out an Estimate of What You Will Need

Use the example shown in Table 7.4 to shape your own needs analysis and estimate the working capital necessary for your practice. Be realistic with your estimates. Remember, banks are in the business of lending money so your request for financing should be comprehensive. You will not please your banker by leaving out necessary expenses.

---

* The author gratefully acknowledges the assistance of Judith Aburmishan, CPA, for her help in preparing this section of the chapter.

Table 7.4: Start-Up Costs for a Typical Internal Medicine Practice

Range:	High	Low
Examination/procedure rooms consisting of examination table, chair, stool, mirror, bulletin board, scale, and medical instruments. $12,500 × 4 ($4,000 × 4)	$50,000	($16,000)
Storage room with racks, step stool, vacuum cleaner, ladder, fire extinguisher, and refrigerator. $10,000 × 1 ($3,000 × 1)	$10,000	($3,000)
Business office and office for physicians with desk, credenza, chair, lamps, mirror, phones, bookshelves, computer (leased), printer (two each: laser and dot matrix), copier, fax machine, and file cabinets. $15,000 × 2 ($15,000 × 1)	$30,000	($15,000)
Reception area with chairs, television, VCR, clock, and magazine rack. $5,000 × 1 ($4,000 × 1)	$5,000	($4,000)
Start-up costs consisting of professional fees (legal, accounting, and consulting), printing, newspaper advertising, office supply inventory, medical disposable supply inventory, application fees for health plans, registration fees for license, and rental deposits. $25,000 × 1 ($15,000 × 1)	$25,000	($15,000)
Subtotal:	$120,000	($53,000)
Estimated leasehold improvements not made part of monthly rental payments.	$30,000	($30,000)
Three months working capital requirements. $20,000 × 1, $15,000 × 1, and $10,000 × 1*	$45,000	($45,000)
Total:	$195,000	($128,000)

* Assumes cost to operate equals $20,000 per month less collections received during the second and third months of operation.

It is common for practices to take six months or longer to break even. The estimates above do not take into consideration the particular physicians' personal requirements. If each partner requires $10,000 per month of gross personal income to meet such obligations, the estimates would need to be revised upward.

It is always better to receive a bank commitment for more money than you ultimately need than to run short of funds and request additional financing when the checkbook is empty.

Putting It All Together

The common problems physicians face when establishing a group practice such as compensation planning, distribution of equity, and governance issues require as much art as science to resolve. Unfortunately, there are few right or wrong answers to these issues. Find good partners. Those that share your clinical philosophy toward the practice as well as compliment your family values are essential to success. Talk early and often—without advisors—to determine if a threshold level of willingness to practice together exists among you. Determine whether or not the group members are interested in pooling all resources and sharing equally in the benefit and burdens of the practice. Likewise, flush out the personal interests of all potential partners to determine if lifestyle issues will dominate the practice. Should every practice have a commander-in-chief, or is governing by committee the most effective method of control? You cannot possibly answer any of these questions incorrectly if your answers match those of your partners.

Finally, once agreement is reached, do yourself a favor and put the understandings in written form. It will assuredly save you time and expense later.

Self-Test: What Is the Right Way for You?

Business Organization

1. What are the advantages and disadvantages of sole proprietorship for you?

2. What is the most advantageous way for you to structure a partnership with other physicians?

3. Have you considered creating a professional corporation as the legal structure for your practice?

4. What kinds of governing committees or boards should be set up to manage the partnership?

Offices and Leases

1. What local ordinances or zoning governs where you may situate your offices?

2. Have potential landlords and building managers set out rules and conditions clearly (and have you responded with questions and counterproposals)?

3. Have you had a lawyer versed in real estate matters read your lease?

4. Have you had a disinterested party (such as a space planner) calculate how much square-footage you are actually renting?

5. Have you had an adequate professional such as an architect create an estimate for the buildout?

6. What options and special clauses in the lease would be to your advantage? Have you asked potential landlords to include such options and special clauses in the leases that they prepare for you?

Working Capital

1. Have you calculated how much working capital will be needed while your practice is in its start-up phase?

2. Have you applied for a line of credit at your bank? What other kinds of interim financing are available?

Furnishings

1. Who is preparing the list of furnishings?

2. Who is in charge of creating a budget for the furnishings?

3. Who has approval over moneys spent on furnishings?

Chapter 8

How to Set Up the Finances of Your New Practice

Joel M Blau, CFP and Ronald J Paprocki, JD, CFP

The key factor in achieving true financial independence is planning ahead for your personal well being. The key objectives discussed in Chapter 4 also apply to a decision-making process for the development of your practice of medicine: set clear goals, maximize appropriate tax benefits, and exercise the discipline required to see these goals become a reality.

Setting goals for your new practice requires more than addressing the tax-related or law-related issues. These goals should complement the personal objectives you may have established for your new lifestyle. After all, if you are anticipating a substantial amount of time to pursue non-medical activities, it does not make sense to structure your new career in medicine as a solo practitioner where you can anticipate being on call twenty-four hours a day. Too often, physicians assume that they can manage a full schedule of treating patients and pursuing non-medical activities. When doing so, we often find that the physician disappoints patients, business colleagues, family members, or others who expected to play a more important role in the life of the "new" physician.

While goal setting relates to many of the non-financial issues, care should be given to the elements that can make your financial picture more advantageous. Depending on the type of business structure you choose, many fringe benefits may be provided on a tax-advantaged basis. This can enable the practice to enhance your personal well being. For example, incorporating your practice will help to protect your personal assets from potential claims made against your employees and allow for the tax deductibility of limited amounts of health care coverage or life insurance protection. (Incorporation, though, does not protect you from professional liability exposure.)

Finally, a strong sense of discipline is required to make certain that you can remain on course throughout this time so that personal and practice objectives can be met. Successful accomplishments in these areas require a substantial commitment to a disciplined process.

In this chapter, we focus on the elements vital to your financial health and your change of medical career. In particular, we examine three key steps to maximize the benefits that can be provided by a medical practice:

- Planning investment strategies for your future
- Constructing an insurance portfolio
- Selecting a qualified retirement plan

Investment Planning

Whether you are setting up a retirement plan or interested in only monitoring your personal account, it helps to have a general understanding of how to structure an investment portfolio. With this knowledge, you will be better prepared to make decisions that will lead to your financial independence. Figure 8.1 illustrates a typical investment-planning process.

Background: Selecting a Productive Portfolio

Before you can effectively follow the process outlined in Figure 8.1, some education is required. There are three generally accepted determinants that affect the performance of a portfolio: security selection, market timing, and portfolio construction.

The first determinant, *security selection,* relates to the specific stock, bond, or mutual fund chosen. You have probably made security selections based on information gathered through publications or other public information sources. If your experience is similar to many physicians, you have probably received your fair share of tips about possible opportunities.

Figure 8.1: A Systematic and Proven Investment Process

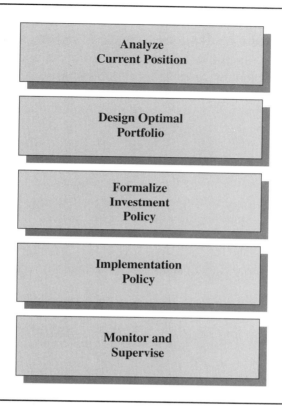

The second determinant, *market timing,* refers to executing the purchase or sale of an investment at a specific time based on various technical indicators. Graphs and trendlines are used in this strategy to determine various points in time for purchases and sales. Generally, investors hope to buy before prices increase and sell before prices decline.

The third determinant, *portfolio construction,* refers to asset class selection—how much of the portfolio is invested in United States stocks, international stocks, bonds, or cash. Stock can be further divided into Large Company and Small Company. Bonds can be long-term, medium-term, or short-term maturities, or high quality or high yield (lower quality).

Several studies have been conducted over varying time periods to quantify the importance of security selection, market timing, and asset class selection on a portfolio's overall return. The most widespread study was conducted by Brinson, Singer, and Beebower.[1] Their study looked at institutional money management for large retirement plans and bank trust companies over two different ten-year periods. It was determined that security selection accounted for only 4% of the portfolio's return. Market timing, that is, making decisions based on technical indicators or other forecasting techniques, accounted for 2% of the portfolio's return.

Researchers found that 94% of the portfolio's total return was a function of asset allocation. While most investors spend nearly all of their time focusing on market timing or security selection, the studies suggest that asset allocation is the key to constructing a successful portfolio. If you are like most people, you are spending the majority of your time on security selection, and possibly a significant amount of time on market timing, while completely discounting the importance of asset class selection.

Now that you have the foundation of investment planning theory, let's further develop the process that can assist you to achieve success.

Analyze Current Position

The first step is to determine how your assets are combined and allocated within your total portfolio. Your current asset allocation strategy may not be the result of careful planning and implementation. We regularly review investment holdings that derive from an investment "strategy" consisting of individual decisions made on the spur of the moment, with little information available, and usually based on fleeting emotions. This is not a good way to plan for long-term success.

You can develop a better idea of where you are by dividing your investments among the asset classes of large domestic companies, small domestic companies, international companies, bonds, and cash. The resulting percentages will give you insight into how much risk you may be taking for the expected return you may achieve. It is important to make certain that you are not taking excessive risk based on your own subjective tolerances.

To provide perspective, some sample asset-allocation strategies and their risk-reward characteristics are shown in Table 8.1. Return and loss statistics have been rounded to illustrate the impact of different amounts of asset classes.

Table 8.1: Asset-Allocation Strategies

Portfolio Consisting of:	Expected 5-Year Annual Return	Possible 1-Year Loss
Large Companies: 25%		
Small Companies: 0%		
International Companies: 5%	8.6%	-7.5%
Bonds: 67%		
Cash: 3%		
Large Companies: 41%		
Small Companies: 5%		
International Companies: 14%	10%	-10%
Bonds: 37%		
Cash: 3%		
Large Companies: 49%		
Small Companies: 11%		
International Companies: 19%	11%	-12.5%
Bonds: 18%		
Cash: 3%		

Source: MEDIQUS Asset Advisors, Inc.

Use Asset Allocation to Design Your Optimal Portfolio

What is the appropriate process to follow in building a portfolio? The key in investment planning is to minimize short-term risk while maximizing long-term gain. Often, we review physicians' portfolios that can produce an unnecessary amount of risk given the expected rate of return. The important question to answer for your portfolio is "How much short-term risk are you willing to endure for the long-term benefit of your investment portfolio?"

The risk-reward ratio implies that to achieve a higher rate of return, you must assume a higher level of risk. However, that is not necessarily so. Figure 8.2 illustrates the various asset classes and past range of returns within a 12-month period.

Viewing the range of returns chart in Figure 8.2, you can see that the asset classes with the highest long-term rates of return also have the highest amount of short-term risk. Think of risk as *fluctuation*. How much will that asset fluctuate over time to achieve those average rates of return? How

Figure 8.2: Asset Class and Associated Risk

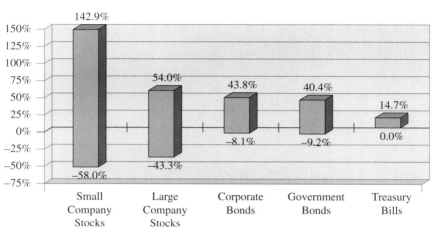

Range of Yearly Returns for Asset Classes, 1925-99

much fluctuation are you comfortable with to achieve your target average rate of return?

Effective asset allocation can create a balance within your portfolio. By placing your capital in a variety of asset classes, each component is designed to act in a specific way within your portfolio.

Stocks offer the potential to earn attractive returns, but they entail more short-term risk than some other types of investments. Bonds generally provide more stability than equities (stocks). By including both bonds and equities in your portfolio, you seek to balance your portfolio. Cash assets, such as money-market accounts, offer liquidity and a convenient "parking place" for cash for future investment opportunities.

Modern Portfolio Theory: A Framework for Asset Allocation

Another important concept in the asset-allocation process is modern portfolio theory. The 1990 Nobel Prize in Economic Sciences was awarded to three economists for their work in developing modern portfolio theory—a framework that is important in the efficient management of an investment portfolio. The three basic premises of modern portfolio theory are worth-while considering in detail:

- **Markets are efficient.** Over time, it is difficult for an individual investor to consistently "beat the market." Technology has created an environment that makes information instantly available to a potentially limitless number of investors.

- **Attention should be focused on the investment portfolio as a whole rather than on individual investments that make up the portfolio.** As previously illustrated, studies have shown that more than 90% of the impact of an investment portfolio is a result of the selection of asset classes rather than the selection of a particular security or market timing. Therefore, so much of the energy spent trying to pick or time the purchase of the "best" stock, bond, or mutual fund is wasted. Individual investors would be much better off deciding on and monitoring specific asset-class selection among domestic and international asset classes.

- **At any given level of risk, there is a particular combination of asset classes that will maximize return.** Therefore, not only is the selection of the type of asset class important, but also the determination of the amount to be invested in each class will help to maximize return at a given level of risk.

There are two ways to reduce risk. One is through diversification. The other is time. Your investment time frame may be long term (retirement), medium term (college funding), or short term (purchasing a new home). If the investment time period is less than three to five years, the appropriate strategy is to invest primarily in fixed income (bonds) and cash equivalents (money markets, certificates of deposit, or treasury bills). If, however, the time period is expected to exceed three to five years, investing a portion of assets in equities is reasonable. Periods of longer than five years have provided a much lower level of volatility for stocks.

Once you define your investment goals and determine a time frame, you can create a diversified portfolio by combining various asset classes. To illustrate reducing risk using asset allocation, we should view historical data and sample portfolios. Let's look at the investment plan of a typical ultraconservative physician. He has decided to invest all of his assets in United States government bonds. He knows that these bonds are guaranteed to return his principal at maturity as well as provide him with a guaranteed fixed rate of return.

Looking at United States government bonds on the asset class and risk chart (Figure 8.3), we see that the risk associated is higher than that of treasury bills, but it is lower than all of the equity classes. Even though bonds are guaranteed, they can fluctuate in value. Further, bond values move inversely to interest rates. Interest rate changes cause the price of government bonds to change. If you sell the bond before to maturity, you may not receive your full principal since interest rate changes may have caused the price of the bond to fall. This fluctuation is reflected in the risk level of this asset class. Regardless of these fluctuations, this ultraconservative physician is satisfied with this investment, which is shown as Portfolio A in Figure 8.3.

Let's compare this conservative approach against a diversified portfolio. Three diversified portfolios are shown in Figure 8.3. Note the column titled "Risk." This number identifies the possible fluctuation from the expected return over any twelve-month period. For example, a risk of 11.7% for Portfolio A can produce a maximum performance of 16.7% (expected return of 5% plus fluctuation of 11.7%) or can produce a minimum one year return of -6.7% (expected return of 5% minus 11.7%). Risk is often expressed as standard deviation, which also includes an assumption of the likelihood of the range of return falling within the expressed estimate of fluctuation.

Note the risk figure associated with government bonds (Portfolio A). By adding U.S. blue chip stocks as well as cash assets, we can structure a portfolio that actually provides a higher expected rate of return with the same level of risk (Portfolio C). If the investor is not comfortable with this blend, the portfolio can be adjusted to have the same level of return but with less risk (Portfolio B).

Concentrating on asset class enables you to structure a portfolio and be relatively confident of its overall risk as well as its projected long-term return. A number of computer software programs can aid you in asset-allocation number crunching. Many financial advisors can also help you in the proper structuring of a portfolio based on your specific risk-return parameters.

Figure 8.3: Diversification and the Risk/Return Tradeoff

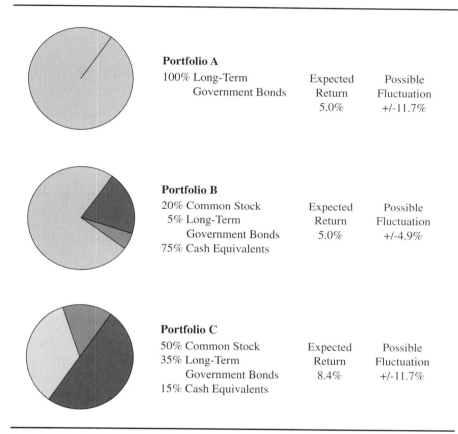

Portfolio A

100% Long-Term
     Government Bonds

Expected	Possible
Return	Fluctuation
5.0%	+/-11.7%

Portfolio B

20% Common Stock
 5% Long-Term
     Government Bonds
75% Cash Equivalents

Expected	Possible
Return	Fluctuation
5.0%	+/-4.9%

Portfolio C

50% Common Stock
35% Long-Term
     Government Bonds
15% Cash Equivalents

Expected	Possible
Return	Fluctuation
8.4%	+/-11.7%

Think about your own investment plan. Are you spending the majority of time on issues that add little to the bottom line, such as market timing or specific stock selection? Most investors do. Every day physicians buy into the hot tip because it is being promoted as a money-making, "sure thing." They do this without a thought about its place in their portfolio. If you need to buy this hot stock or take advantage of a tip, do it with limited funds that you have set aside for such risk taking. Do it only *after* you have set up a truly diversified, well-funded portfolio, not at the expense of a diversified investment plan.

Formalize Your Investment Policy

The next step in the investment process can eliminate future second-guessing or confusion about decisions made in the past. Simply stated, it is important to formalize your investment policy by documenting the decisions that you made for the account in question. This can best be accomplished through the use of an *investment policy statement.* Such a document will identify the allocation strategy to be followed, the expected rate of return, and the possible one-year risk. It can also identify the specific investments chosen for your portfolio.

The primary benefit of this step is to keep you from straying when future investment issues are presented. Rather than being side-tracked into areas that will not serve your long-term needs, you can rely on the policy statement to keep you focused.

Implementation Policy

Once you have focused on the most important determinant of a portfolio's performance —asset-class selection —you can structure a portfolio that will meet your needs. After deciding how your portfolio should be allocated among the various asset classes, you can begin funding your investment plan.

Not surprisingly, we believe there is a process that you should follow to begin implementing your investment plan. First, you should determine the length of time that your assets will be invested. For example, are you setting aside assets that you will need in two months or in twenty years? If your needs are short term, you should look at the more liquid assets that we discussed earlier in this chapter. Long-term needs are more likely to require ownership assets.

If the time period is expected to be less than five years, investing primarily in fixed-income investments (such as bonds) and cash equivalents (such as money markets or treasury bills) is appropriate. Generally, stocks are not appropriate as the volatility of stocks can be significant over such a short time. (If the time will exceed five years, investing a portion of the portfolio in stocks would be reasonable, as periods of time greater than five years have traditionally provided a much lower level of volatility for stocks.)

The second step is to determine what asset classes should be considered for the portfolio. Should you include small domestic companies and international or emerging markets? The third step is to determine the amount you will feel comfortable having invested in each asset class.

The final step relates to product selection. Earlier in this chapter we described the major investment vehicles that are used in a portfolio. At this point in the planning process, you must decide if you are going to use individual stocks and bonds or mutual funds. Because of the advantages of diversification and continuous professional management, mutual funds are often used to develop an investment portfolio.

Monitor and Supervise

The final step to a successful process is to inspect what you expect. Simply stated, you should regularly review the performance of your investments, the expenses incurred with your portfolio, and the services provided by your advisors.

Ask if the performance results have lived up to expectations. Short-term results can vary substantially from expectations. It is important at least to compare investment performance with the respective index benchmark.

Expenses should also be reviewed to determine if the expected expenses have been exceeded by actual results. If so, you need to ask if unnecessary costs have resulted from excessive transactions or undisclosed fees. Service expectations should also be monitored to make certain that advisors have been delivering the value-added benefits that were promised before you became a client.

Constructing an Insurance Portfolio

In Chapter 3, we discussed the importance of hazard protection. You should make sure that in the event of death or disability you have implemented risk-management programs that will assist the continuance of the practice and guarantee that your family will be well provided for.

Insurance plays a critical role in any risk-management discussion. Just as you insure your automobile and home, you also need to insure yourself and thus protect your ability to earn an income. The insurance industry provides a multitude of products to address your needs: disability insurance, business overhead insurance, disability buyout insurance, and various life-insurance programs, including term, whole life, universal life, and variable universal life insurance.

When constructing an insurance portfolio, make sure it is structured around your own needs. For example, the first step is to identify the possible hazards from which you require protection. Is your concern centered on the possibility of a malpractice claim? Or career-ending disability? Or sudden death? For each of these possible hazards, you should try to determine what amount of income would be required for you or your survivors to maintain a desired standard of living. How long should the income be provided? Would there be any possible source of income for the family? What rate of inflation should be assumed? What rate of return on investment assets should be assumed? The answers to these questions can help you to make intelligent insurance purchases.

In addition, your answers to the questions that follow can also provide a starting off point to help you assess your personal situation and determine where additional risk coverage may be required.

Asset Protection

- Are assets owned outside of your retirement plan titled in your name or joint titled between you and your spouse?

- Is your medical practice organized as a sole proprietorship or partnership?

- Do you have any employees in your medical practice?

- Do you or your spouse own a business that is not incorporated?

- Does this business have any employees or equal shareholders?

- Do you volunteer or serve as a director for any charitable organizations?

- Is your specialty one that is likely to be the subject of a lawsuit?

If you answered *yes* to any of these questions, you should review your malpractice coverage, umbrella insurance policies (those covering your personal as well as professional activities), and asset-protection strategies with a competent advisor.

Disability

- Can you financially afford to retire today?

- Can you leave your practice for an extended period of time and not experience a substantial loss of personal net income?

- Do you have a substantial source of income that is independent of your ability to practice? If so, would this income be available even if you cannot work at this activity?

If you answered *no* to any of these questions, you need to protect one of your most important financial assets: your ability to produce income. The answers to the following questions will help to identify your needs:

- How much does your family spend after taxes each month to maintain its current lifestyle?

- What monthly expenses would be eliminated if you were disabled?

- What monthly expenses would be created if you were disabled?

- What is the total amount of assets that can be used to produce income for you in the event of a disability?

- What amount of cash reserve "emergency fund" do you maintain?

- Would you expect your spouse to work in the event you were unable to practice medicine?

If your assets would not be able to support your required standard of living for a reasonable time period, you should review your current disability coverage, office overhead coverage (insurance that provides additional income to cover the costs of operating your practice), and disability buyout coverage (insurance that can provide a substantial cash amount for the purpose of purchasing an interest in a practice).

In the Event of Your Death

- How much does your family spend after taxes each month to maintain its current lifestyle?

- Compared to your current after-tax monthly standard of living, what amount (if any) could be eliminated in the event of your death?

- Over what amount of time is this income required?

- Which assets do you currently own that could be converted into income-producing assets in the event of your death?

- Is there any source of income that your family could depend on in the event of your death?

- Would you expect your spouse to work in the event of your death?

- How much income could your spouse reasonably earn?

- Would you expect to satisfy the estimated educational expense estimates for your children in the event of your death?

These questions can help to identify whether there is a financial need for your family in the event of your death. One of the most commonly asked questions is, "How much capital (or life insurance) should I have to support my family if I die?" The answer will depend on the answers to the preceding questions as well as on the assumptions relating to long-term asset requirements: What rate of return should you reasonably expect on the assets available to produce income? What rate of inflation should you anticipate?

For example, assuming a 4% rate of inflation, you need a certain amount of assets to provide $1,000 of monthly purchasing power. The total amount required also depends on the rate of return earned on the capital and the length of time the monthly income is required (see Table 8.2).

Table 8.2: Capital Required to Produce $1,000 of Monthly Purchasing Power for Different Time Periods at Different Rates of Return, Assuming 4% Inflation

Number of Years Income Required	6% Rate of Return	8% Rate of Return	10% Rate of Return
10	$108,226	$98,080	$89,295
15	$155,082	$134,867	$118,325
20	$197,681	$165,328	$140,255
25	$236,411	$190,551	$156,822

The key is to work with an advisor who fully understands what you would like to accomplish in protecting your most important financial asset—your earning ability. A portfolio of insurance coverage can then be structured to protect you from death and disability. Make sure that your insurance adviser works along with your accountant to maximize the tax advantages of how you pay premiums as well as the tax ramifications of receiving those benefits.

Once you have addressed and implemented an efficient risk-management program, you will want to look further into ways the practice can compliment your long-term goals.

Retirement Plans

In the past, physicians planned for retirement by reviewing a potentially expansive list of income sources, such as Social Security, pensions from health-care organizations, and income from a variety of investment portfolios. Today, planning for retirement income has become much more focused on the areas that the physician is able to control and contribute. For example, it is now appropriate to ask the question of whether Social Security will be available for retirement income. It is becoming more important to plan well in advance for the income needs that will exist during retirement.

One of the greatest benefits of any business is the ability to contribute on a tax-deductible basis to retirement plans. When the business is your own practice, you will choose the plan that can most benefit your own personal situation as well as creating long-term incentives for your employees.

As more physicians become aware of their own need to plan for future income security, qualified retirement plans remain the logical starting point. Qualified retirement plans are generally classified as "defined benefit" or "defined contribution." Some plans may combine features of both types.

Defined-Benefit Plans

Defined-benefit plans tend to favor older, highly compensated employees, such as a physician who is close to retirement. That is because more of the employer's contributions must go into his or her account to compensate for the relatively short time period before retirement. Actuarial calculations are used to estimate how much must be contributed each year to accumulate the necessary future amount. Interest rates, investment rates of return, and the age of participants will have an impact on the calculation. The investment risk rests solely on the employer. The employer is required to fund the plan adequately each year, although the annual contribution can vary based on the plan's investment results. The future benefit received may be based on a flat percentage of compensation, a percentage that increases with the length of service, a percentage that changes at certain compensation levels, or a number of other formulas.

There are many advantages to the employees. First, the plan is completely funded by the employer, and neither the contributions nor earnings are taxed to the employee. Also, the employee has peace of mind knowing he or she will receive a future benefit. Many plans will even allow an employee to borrow from the plan within certain strict guidelines.

The primary disadvantage of a defined-benefit plan relates to younger plan participants. Younger employees generally receive a smaller portion of the total contribution, primarily because of the longer time period before their retirement.

From an employer's standpoint, some advantages of a defined-benefit plan include:

- The ability to reward long-term employees with a substantial retirement benefit even though they are close to retirement age

- Forfeitures from terminating employees that reduce future funding requirements for current employees

- Plan investments directed solely by the employer

Although it was once the qualified retirement plan of choice for many medical practices, the defined-benefit plan has become much less popular because of the following employer disadvantages:

- In low-profit years, the employer is still obligated to make plan contributions.

- Investment risk rests solely with the employer.

- Administration costs are higher than for defined-contribution plans because an actuary must be retained to certify the reasonableness of the contribution and deduction.

Defined-Contribution Plans

There are several variations of defined-contribution plans commonly used by small medical practices: Money Purchase Pension Plans, Profit-Sharing Plans, Age Weighted Profit-Sharing Plans, and "SIMPLE" Plans.

Money Purchase Pension Plan In a Money Purchase Pension Plan, the employer contributes a specified percentage of the total participating employees' salaries each year. This contribution is allocated among the participants. Up to 25% of the participants' payroll can be contributed and deducted by the employer. Plan contributions can be based on total compensation, including bonuses and overtime pay. Maximum recognized compensation for 2001 is $170,000. This amount is indexed for inflation, but only in increments of $10,000; therefore, the limit increases only when the sum of the inflation adjustments equals or exceeds $10,000. Thus, a participant's annual account contribution may not exceed the lesser of 25% of compensation or $35,000 per year.

Money purchase pension plans typically favor younger participants because they have a longer time period over which their accounts will grow. In many instances, they will share in plan forfeitures. Forfeitures occur when participants leave the practice before they have become 100% vested. The nonvested forfeitures are then reallocated to the remaining participants, thus benefiting employees who remain in the plan the longest.

In addition to the deductibility of the contributions, there are other advantages for the employer, including the following:

- Contributions, as well as administrative costs, are known in advance.

- Contributions will rise as compensation rises, but they are controllable both by formula and absolute dollar amounts.

- The employer can direct the investment portfolio, or the employees can self-direct their own portions of the plan.

The primary disadvantage to the employer stems from mandatory contributions. The employer is obligated to make contributions, even in years when the practice loses money. The primary disadvantage to the employee is the lack of a guarantee of the amount of retirement benefit, as the investment risk rests on the employee participant regardless of who directs the investments.

Profit-Sharing Plans For greater employer flexibility, a profit-sharing plan may be the defined-contribution plan of choice. Employer contributions to the plan need not be made every year. The maximum annual deduction is limited to 15% of compensation, with an individual recognized maximum compensation of $170,000 (as of 2001).

Although annual contributions are generally discretionary, if there are profits, the employer is expected to make "substantial and recurring" contributions. As a rule of thumb, contributions in three out of five years or five out of ten years will usually satisfy the IRS.

For employees, profit-sharing plans favor younger participants. However, the down sides of a profit-sharing plan are similar to a money purchase plan. There are no guarantees of the amount of future retirement benefits, and the investment risk rests on the employee. In addition, there is no assurance of the frequency and amount of employer contributions.

Advantages of a profit-sharing plan to the employer include:

- The plan gives an incentive to employees to be productive to maximize the profit potential of the practice.

- Contributions are totally flexible.

- Forfeitures of terminating employees are reallocated among active participants, generally with a greater percentage allocated to the highest salaried participants, such as the physicians.

Because contribution limits of profit-sharing plans are set at 15% of covered payroll, however, this type of plan will generally not produce as large a contribution and deduction for older employees when compared to a defined-benefit plan.

Age-Weighted Profit-Sharing Plans Because defined-contribution plans tend to favor younger employees, another alternative is the age-weighted profit-sharing plan. Employer contributions in this type of plan are not necessarily based on profits. The contributions are totally flexible and at the discretion of the employer. Contributions need not be made yearly, so long as they are "substantial and recurring." Employer contributions are allocated to provide an equal retirement benefit at normal retirement age for all participants. Older participants are favored from a contribution perspective since they are closer to retirement. However, all participants would receive the same projected retirement benefit percentage at age sixty-five. Age-weighted profit-sharing plans do have some potential disadvantages for the employer, including the following:

- If the key employees are younger than other employees, they will not receive as large a proportion of employer contributions.

- Administrative costs are higher because of actuarial calculations.

- It is more difficult to explain the plan to employees.

Any profit-sharing or stock-bonus plan that meets the requirements of Internal Revenue Code 401(k) can be a cash or deferred plan. An employee can agree to a salary reduction or to defer a bonus, although certain participation requirements will apply.

"SIMPLE" Plans The Small Business Job Protection Act of 1996 created an entirely new type of retirement plan called *SIMPLE,* an acronym for *Savings Incentive Match Plan for Employee.* SIMPLE replaces the salary-reduction version of the Simplified Employee Pension, also known as SARSEP. The SIMPLE enables small-business owners to put aside money easily and inexpensively in tax-deferred accounts for both themselves and their employees.

To take advantage of this new form of retirement savings, the business entity must have no more than one hundred employees and cannot use any other retirement plan in the same year. Also, eligible employees must have earned at least $5,000 in any two previous years from the same employer and be likely to do so in the current year.

SIMPLEs are available in two forms: SIMPLE individual retirement account and a SIMPLE 401(k). SIMPLE IRAs can be set up for each employee at minimal cost at a bank, mutual-fund company, or brokerage. SIMPLE 401(k) plans are more expensive mainly because of administrative costs.

SIMPLEs enables owners and employees to defer a percentage of their compensation, up to $6,500 a year, indexed for inflation. Owners may contribute to employees' plans either by matching 3% of participating workers' annual compensation dollar for dollar to a maximum of $6,500 or by contributing 2% of compensation up to $3,000 for all workers, whether or not they participate.

Because the SIMPLE is a new form of retirement plan, many options must be considered before implementation. On the positive side, SIMPLEs require no discrimination testing (which requires a certain relation between the amount of compensation deferred by the group of participants included in the lower level of compensation and those in the higher level of compensation), and employees need not participate for a business owner to defer up to $6,500 plus the 3% match per year. The traditional 401(k) plan limits an employer's tax deferral by the amount employees put into the plan. In addition, the employer has no fiduciary responsibility for employee investments under the SIMPLE arrangement.

The physician who wants to save more for retirement and take a bigger deduction may find the maximum contribution confining. Other qualified plans allow an employer to deduct as much as 25% of their salary up to $35,000 per year. Also, because SIMPLE money is fully vested from the beginning, the plan provides little incentive for employee loyalty. Table 8.3 recaps many of the basic issues in qualified plan alternatives and should assist you in understanding the differences among plans.

Table 8.3: Qualified Plans Compared

Feature	Defined-Benefit Plans	Defined-Contribution Plans			
	All Defined-Benefit Plans	Money Purchase Pension	Profit-Sharing	Age-Weighted Profit-Sharing	SIMPLE
Employer contributions deductible?	Yes	Yes	Yes	Yes	Yes
Employer contributions to participant currently taxable?	No	No	No	No	No
Earnings accumulate with income tax deferred?	Yes	Yes	Yes	Yes	Yes
Maximum annual employer contribution or deduction?	Determined by actuary	25% of compensation	15% of compensation	15% of compensation	Match up to 3% of compensation or 2% of compensation of all eligible employees
Employer contributions required?	Yes	Yes	No	No	Yes
Employer contribution is allocated:	N/A	1. As a percentage of total covered compensation 2. Integrated with Social Security	1. As a percentage of total covered compensation 2. Integrated with Social Security	Based on number of years before participant reaches retirement age	Pro-rata by compensation
Employee contributions required?	No	No	No	No	No

Table 8.3: Qualified Plans Compared (continued)

Feature	Defined-Benefit Plans	Defined-Contribution Plans			
	All Defined-Benefit Plans	Money Purchase Pension	Profit-Sharing	Age-Weighted Profit-Sharing	SIMPLE
Maximum participant benefits (for defined- benefit plans) or allocations (for defined-contribution plans)	Lesser of 100% of compensation or $140,000 annually	Lesser of 25% of compensation or $35,000	Lesser of 25% of compensation or $35,000	Lesser of 25% of compensation or $35,000	Lesser of 100% of compensation or $12,000
Investments can be self -directed by participants?	No	Yes	Yes	Yes	Yes
What plan participants are favored by the plan design?	Older, closer to retirement, highly compensated	Highly compensated	Highly compensated	Older, closer to retirement, highly compensated	Younger
What will participant's account value at retirement depend on?	Formula of the plan, which can be calculated based on: years before retirement, compensation, years of service	The amount of contributions The number of years until retirement Investment return	Frequency and amount of contributions Number of years until retirement Investment return	Frequency and amount of contributions Number of years until retirement Investment return	Frequency and amount of contributions Number of years until retirement Investment return
Who bears investment risk?	Employer	Employee	Employee	Employee	Employee

What Plan May Be Right for You?

There are many factors to consider when evaluating different types of retirement plans for your practice. Table 8.4 can help you to evaluate the benefits of each and narrow the alternatives. Be certain to consult with your retirement experts before making a final decision.

Table 8.4: Evaluating Retirement Plans

Plan Type	If you need flexibility in making deposits	If you would be the oldest, most highly compensated, or closest to retirement of all participants	If you would be able to afford contributions that would exceed 25% of participant compensation
Defined Benefit	Do not consider	Definitely consider	Definitely consider
Money Purchase Pension	Do not consider	Consider	No impact
Profit-Sharing	Definitely consider	Unlikely to consider	Consider
Age-Weighted Profit-Sharing	Definitely consider	Definitely consider	Consider
SIMPLE Plan	Definitely consider	Unlikely to consider	Unlikely to consider

Implementing Your Plan

Many skilled professionals are available to assist with qualified-plan implementation. A third-party administrator helps in plan design, participant information, and tax reporting. The trustees can take responsibility for investing or can hire an investment manager. An actuary will be involved when using defined-benefit plans or age-weighted profit-sharing plans. Many professional financial organizations can act in multiple capacities. For smaller plans, the practice's accountants may perform the duties of plan administration, while the principal physicians act as trustees and hire investment professionals to construct and invest the portfolio. Whatever group or entity the medical practice chooses to work with, they must be aware of the goals and objectives that the practice has determined to be in its best interest.

Regardless of the type of plan chosen, care must be taken to observe the various tax and legal requirements established by the IRS and the Department of Labor. IRS regulations require the filing of the appropriate tax forms for the plan, such as Form 5500, which reports on the assets, contributions, and expenses of the plan. Your accountant or Third Party Administrator usually handles these administrative matters. Department of Labor requirements include the distribution of required information to plan participants, making distributions to former participants in a timely fashion, and other miscellaneous items.

There is a separate item that falls under the Department of Labor domain: the need to satisfy a variety of requirements regarding the investment of plan assets. To assist plan trustees, a series of requirements have been identified in the Employees Retirement Income Security Act commonly known as ERISA. These requirements are:

- An investment policy must be established and should be in writing. (ERISA Sections 402(a)(1), 40229(b)(1) to (2), 404(a)(1)(D))

- Plan assets must be diversified. (ERISA Section 404(a)(1)(c))

- Investment decisions must be made with the skill and care of a "prudent expert." (ERISA Section 404(a)(1)(b))

- Investment performance must be monitored.(ERISA Section 405(a))

- Investment expenses must be controlled. (ERISA Section 404(a))

- Prohibited transactions must be avoided. (ERISA Section 404(a) and (b))

These requirements make it important for qualified-plan trustees to have a general understanding of investments. The allocation of the plan's investment portfolio should be based on many criteria, including the age of the participants, the plan's risk parameters, the plan's expected liabilities, and the type of plan being used.

Self-Test: Asset Protection

1. Is your medical practice organized as a sole proprietorship or partnership?

2. Do you have any employees in your medical practice?

3. Do you or your spouse own a business that is not incorporated?

4. Does this business have any employees or equal shareholders?

5. Do you volunteer or serve as a director for any charitable organization?

6. Is your specialty one in which you are likely to be subject of a lawsuit?

7. Are any assets that you own held in your name alone, or are they jointly held by you and your spouse?

A Simple Scoring Method: A *yes* answer to any of the first six questions indicates that you are at risk. For example, if your practice is not incorporated, you may find yourself legally responsible for injuries to employees and financial defaults by your partners. If you work with a charitable organization, you should determine to what extent you may be held liable for your actions as a volunteer or board member. Answering yes to one of the first six questions should be a warning to consult with your lawyer about possible legal liability and how to protect yourself from it. You may also have to work with your accountant, insurance agent, or financial planner to create a safe structure for your assets. The answer to question 7 is more complicated. If you hold all assets in your name alone, you may be creating estate-planning problems and unintentionally increasing your spouse's tax burden should you die. On the other hand, it may not be advisable to hold all assets jointly. Consult your lawyer or accountant if you are unsure.

References

1. Brinson BGP, Singer BD, Beebower GL. Determinants of portfolio performance. *Financial Analysts Journal.* May-June 1991:47.

Chapter 9

Setting Up a Practice the Right Way

Peter S Moskowitz, MD

Personal Tasks

As you prepare to establish a new medical practice, whether in partnership with others, as a solo practitioner, or in a multispecialty clinic or a health maintenance organization (HMO) setting, the single most important task in planning is to clarify your professional and personal values.

Clarify Personal Values

Our personal values serve as a rudder in stormy seas. Given an expectation of continuous change and turmoil in healthcare, we need to be solidly grounded in who we are and what is important if we are to establish a consistently supportive work environment. The professional values that we choose serve to form the boundaries around which we make work and service commitments. Our personal values not only reinforce our professional values, but in addition give us direction and clarity in setting priorities for our personal and family lives and relationships.

Not uncommon, physicians find that the values that are important to them personally at mid-career have changed since they were in college or medical school. However, they may not have consciously reconsidered them since that time. As a result, they may be leading their lives and making decisions based on outdated paradigms. Personal values can be divided into two principal categories: personal passions and personal purpose.

Define Your Personal Passions

Fredric M Hudson, PhD, espouses the belief that there are six basic human passions with which we measure our lives; and that for most successful adults, roughly three of these passions are operative at any given developmental stage of adult life.[1,2] These passions are listed in Table 9.1.

As you move into a new practice environment or make a new career choice, consider this list of passions and decide which three are of greatest personal importance. The formula will be unique for every person and will change over time, necessitating periodic reassessment. These passions provide the "juice" of life, the energy with which to drive one's plans for the future. Becoming clear about your personal choice of passions is necessary to properly align your work environment with your personal values. If they are parallel and mutually supportive, you will be much more likely to achieve personal and professional happiness and to have the energy to move forward successfully.

Table 9.1: Core Personal Passions*

Personal Power:	*Claiming Yourself*
Self-esteem; self-confidence; self-nurturing; positive sense of self; clear boundaries; sense of freedom and autonomy.	
Achievement:	*Proving Yourself*
Reaching goals; conducting projects; having ambition; getting results and recognition; winning; doing; making a difference.	
Intimacy:	*Sharing Yourself*
Loving; bonding; caring; being a friend; touching; making relationships work; feeling close; nesting; coupling; parenting.	
Play & Creativity:	*Expressing Yourself*
Being imaginative; intuitive; playful; spontaneous; original; expressive; humorous; artistic; celebrative; curious; childlike; nonpurposive.	
Search for Meaning:	*Integrating Yourself*
Finding wholeness; unity; integrity; peace; an inner connection to all things; spirituality; trust in the flow of life; inner wisdom; search for soul.	
Compassion & Contribution:	*Giving Yourself*
Improving; helping; transcending yourself; leaving a legacy; bonding with all of humanity; leaving the world a better place; serving; volunteering; social and environmental caring.	

* *Based on the work and materials of Fredric M Hudson, PhD, in* The Adult Years: Mastering the Art of Self-Renewal *and* LifeLaunch, A Passionate Guide to the Rest of Your Life.[1,2] *Reprinted with permission from The Hudson Institute, www.hudsoninstitute.com.*

You can become more conscious of your choice of passions by writing them down or, perhaps, by keeping a journal about the importance of each in your new practice environment. This helps to keep your career on track. When the new practice environment goes against our personal passions, a "disconnect" happens that eventually will lead to professional dissatisfaction. A simple exercise to clarify your passions for the next chapter in your life is provided in Table 9.2.

Be Clear About Your Personal Purpose

Purpose is the second component of a personal values assessment. Purpose is the compass of our life, the factor that keeps us pointed in the direction of our dreams. Our purpose becomes increasingly important to maintain our direction in response to external pressures and constant change. It, too, is subject to change as we mature and experience life. As with personal passions, purpose also needs to be reassessed and updated periodically for us to remain on track. Table 9.3 provides a purpose checklist that may be used to clarify your purpose and record a statement of purpose. Follow the directions by sorting through the checklist until you have reduced the list of desired purpose statements to a total of no more than ten. These ten statements should reflect what you want more of in your life. They are not

Table 9.2: My Passions Exercise*

Select your top three Passions. For each one, write why that passion is important—why does it "sing" to you? List specific steps you could take to increase these passions in the next chapter of your life.
Passion #1:
Passion #2:
Passion #3:

* Based on the work and materials of Fredric M Hudson, PhD, in The Adult Years: Mastering the Art of Self-Renewal and LifeLaunch, A Passionate Guide to the Rest of Your Life.[1,2] Reprinted with permission from The Hudson Institute, www.hudsoninstitute.com.

just the things you think others would want you to have—or important things you already have enough of in your life.

Table 9.3: Purpose Checklist*

1. Put a check mark in the **1st Sort Column** of those items that are really important to you or are becoming important to you. (Do NOT include "Shoulds!") There are spaces to write-in your own item. 2. Review the checked items and see if there are any themes. 3. Check only the priority items in the **2nd Sort Column**. 4. Check the top 10 items (or less) in the **Top 10 Column**.			
Top 10	**2nd Sort**	**1st Sort**	**PURPOSE**
			Work Satisfaction
			Reach Goals
			Use My Skills and Abilities
			New Training and Learning
			Network and Explore
			Take More Risks
			Reach the Top
			Start My Own Venture
			More Recognition
			More Power and Influence
			Simplify My Life
			More Balance in My Life
			Get Off the Fast Track
			Learn to Say No
			Accept My Limitations
			Freedom From Financial Burdens
			Build Financial Wealth
			More Self Esteem
			Have More Fun
			Adventure and Excitement
			New and Unique Experiences
			Travel—See the World
			Enjoy My Hobbies
			Use My Creativity
			Create An Exciting Retirement
			More Freedom for Me

Table 9.3: Purpose Checklist* (continued)

Top 10	2nd Sort	1st Sort	PURPOSE
			Nurture Myself
			Have Alone Time
			Stay Healthy
			Regular Exercise
			Deepen My Committed Relationship
			Parent with Love and Wisdom
			Be a Close Family
			Create a Home
			Be a Caring Sibling
			Be a Caring Child to My Parents
			Have Close Friends
			Care and Connect with Others
			Deepen my Spirituality
			Become a Whole Person
			Trust Beyond Myself
			Inner Peace
			Inner Wisdom
			Appreciate Beauty
			Feel My Life Counts
			Leave the World a Better Place
			Community Service
			Mentor Others

Reprinted with permission from The Hudson Institute of Santa Barbara, www.hudsoninstitute.com.

Once you have narrowed your selections to ten or fewer, use them to draft a written purpose statement (see Table 9.4). This statement should be no longer than three or four sentences and should incorporate as many as possible of the key purpose words from your checklist selections. The shorter you make your purpose statement, the more effective it is likely to be. A sample purpose statement might read: "I achieve balance in my life by learning to say no, accepting my limitations, staying healthy, having fun, enjoying hobbies, and deepening my spirituality."

Table 9.4: Purpose Statement*

Using your Top 10 items from your Purpose Checklist, write your first draft of a Purpose Statement. Some people just string together their Top 10 items; others use the themes from their Top 10 as their purpose statement. The key is for you to describe the most important life directions for the next stage of your life.

My purpose in the next chapter of my life is: _____

_____

_____

_____

_____

_____

_____

_____

_____

_____

_____

_____

_____

_____

_____

_____

_____

_____

_____

* Based on the work and materials of Fredric M Hudson, PhD, in The Adult Years: Mastering the Art of Self-Renewal *and* LifeLaunch, A Passionate Guide to the Rest of Your Life.[1,2] *Reprinted with permission from The Hudson Institute, www.hudsoninstitute.com.*

Feel free to revise and rework your purpose statement. When you are finished, put a copy of it in your wallet or daily organizer. Use it as a screen saver on your computer. Tape a copy to your bathroom mirror or to your refrigerator, where you can easily see it each day. Use it to assess your choices and decisions, the way you spend your time and your money, and the way you manage your career so that your decisions are always aligned with your purpose.

Establish Values-Based Financial Management

Now that you have clarified your personal purpose and passions for the next chapter of your life, you can put them to good use to provide the foundation for your financial management and planning. Rather than being influenced only by external forces, demands, and stresses, it is important to allocate your scarce resources, money, and time in accordance with what is most important personally. This is called financial planning from the inside out.

A good place to begin is by assessing your income-expense balance. Regardless of whether you live alone or with a spouse or partner, you can do this by keeping a thorough listing of every expense for a three-month period. Include expenses related to food, snacks, gifts, recreation, transportation, child care, donations, loan payment, rent or mortgage payments, utilities, insurance, clothing, and so on. Exclude your medical practice expenses; you will account for them by calculating net practice income. If you live with another person, both you and your spouse or partner must do this work diligently and pool your records.

During the same three months, keep an accurate record of all sources of income. This will include medical practice net income, consulting income, securities investment income, and income-producing property or hobbies.

After three months have passed, compare your total monthly income with your total monthly expenses. The important question is: Am I/are we making more than I am/we are spending? If the answer is yes, congratulate yourself! Many physicians will discover that they have negative cash flow. If you fall within this category, you can now move on to create both short- and long-term financial goals; and you can address the question of how to be more efficient at saving to meet those financial goals.

If, on the other hand, your answer is no, you are spending more than you are making. You have some immediate downsizing to do. Even if your income is expected to increase, you must control your expenses until your income recovers. This is a particularly onerous task. No one enjoys compromising their comfortable lifestyle.

What's more, you and your partner may not agree on how or whether to reduce expenses, which may introduce new power struggles into your relationship. You may encounter numerous internal obstacles and attitudes that prevent you from taking action. Some of those attitudes are listed in Table 9.5.

At times like this, be patient and gentle with yourself and with your partner. Keep the lines of communication open and stay focused on the goal and your purpose. Avoid "blame and shame" statements about individual spending patterns. This is a major challenge for you to meet. In a partnership, arriving at a win-win solution is critical if you and your partner are to reach your future financial goals.

Table 9.5: Roadblocks to Action

Obstacles to Physicians' Financial Downsizing	
INTERNAL OBSTACLES	**FAULTY THINKING**
1. Equating income with worth and skills	Decreasing income means lower self-esteem
2. Linking self-esteem to ability to provide	Decreasing income means failure as a provider
3. Viewing money as a symbol of personal power	Decreasing income means you are powerless, incompetent
4. Spending as a form of self-medicating	Downsizing leads to fear, other "denied" feelings in withdrawal
5. Viewing money as a symbol of sexual potency	Downsizing leads to thoughts of sexual inadequacy
EXTERNAL OBSTACLES	**FAULTY THINKING**
1. Financial over-extension	I deserve my fancy house, car, etc. I am a failure without my…
2. Expectations of spouse	I married you with the expectation of a certain lifestyle; don't stop now. Fear leads to controlling, resistance, manipulation, power struggles
3. Expectations of children/family	You must not love me anymore. I can't be happy without my…
4. Family financial goals assume steady and/or growing income	My services will always be in demand. Medicine is a growth field forever.
5. Marriage/primary relationship may be material-based, not spiritually-based	*Physician:* I am lovable because of my money. *Spouse:* I must marry rich.

When differences of opinion are uncovered, accept them. Neither of you is right or wrong; you simply have different perspectives. Work to secure key compromises on these differences. You may both be required to accept a position that is inferior to what you originally hoped for. Should you be unable to agree, or when goals diverge, self-referral to a qualified couple's therapist or a certified financial planner, or both, may be necessary.

Values-based financial planning also entails short- and long-term planning that addresses and supports your purpose and personal values. Decide what matters most to you and review your purpose statement. Create workable solutions to fund those priorities over time. Such planning usually requires the input and guidance of a certified financial planner.

Establish Values-Based Time Management

Becoming an effective physician means utilizing all of your limited resources effectively, including your time. Although the concept of time management is familiar to all busy professionals, and although most of us have some form of time management tool in use, to become most effective you must use *values-based* time management. In other words, you develop a plan for your time that is based on your own values—and supports those values—rather than spending your time entirely according to the dictates of external factors and the demands of others.

To begin practicing values-based time management, we must first have a simple process of time management. Although there are many time management schemes, one approach that requires no new purchases of books, tapes, or electronic devices is provided in the time-management exercise shown in Table 9.6.

Table 9.6: Time Management Exercise*

You have *168 hours a week*. Knowing that time is one of your most precious resources, analyze how you spend your time in a typical week and how you want to invest your time in the future. Please note *maintenance activities* can span all roles and include activities that seem unnecessary but which do not add value to those roles; some examples: bill paying, house maintenance, etc.

- Identify how many hours you *currently spend* a week on the following:
  - _____ Sleep
  - _____ Maintenance
  - _____ Personal Activities
  - _____ Couple Activities
  - _____ Family Activities
  - _____ Friends Activities
  - _____ Work/Career Activities
  - _____ Community Activities

- Identify how you *plan to invest your weekly time* for your next chapter:
  - _____ Sleep
  - _____ Maintenance
  - _____ Personal Activities
  - _____ Couple Activities
  - _____ Family Activities
  - _____ Friends Activities
  - _____ Work/Career Activities
  - _____ Community Activities

On the pie charts below, use approximate percentages to graphically illustrate the comparison between your current and future time allotment.

For simplicity, 1 Hour = 0.6% of Week.

Current Commitments   **Future Commitments**

* *Based on the work and materials of Fredric M Hudson, PhD, in* The Adult Years: Mastering the Art of Self-Renewal *and* LifeLaunch, A Passionate Guide to the Rest of Your Life.[1,2] *Reprinted with permission from The Hudson Institute, www.hudsoninstitute.com.*

This is a simple activity. To use it, complete the first section by indicating the number of hours per week you typically devote to each activity listed. Multiply each hour total by 0.6 to convert each hourly sum to a percentage of a weekly number.

Once you have calculated a weekly percentage for each activity listed in Table 9.6, create a pie chart, drawing each segment of the pie in proportion to the percentage of a week number you just calculated. The total of all of the segments in your pie chart must equal 100%. This will visually represent the way you currently spend your time each week. Are you pleased with this distribution of your time?

Review this pie chart distribution while looking at the three passions and the ten purpose statements you identified for yourself earlier in this section (see Tables 9.2 and 9.3). Does your current use of time reflect your purpose and passions the way you would like it to? Perhaps this exercise has helped you recognize that you are spending a disproportionate amount of your weekly time in an activity that does not support your personal values. You may find, for example, that you would like to spend more of your time with family or friends—time for yourself. Perhaps you would like to spend less time at work or doing work-related tasks.

Now draw a second pie chart and modify each segment to reflect how you would prefer to spend your time in the next chapter of your life. This revised time wheel represents *values-based time management.* To bring your time management into alignment with your personal and professional values, use this exercise at least once a year to assess exactly how you are budgeting your time. Your personal and professional effectiveness and your happiness naturally improve when your use of time fully supports your own values, rather than those determined arbitrarily by others or through random life circumstances.

It is also important to reassess your time wheel each time you anticipate a major transition in your personal or professional life. This will promote and maximize your own efficient use of time, particularly with regard to reallocating your time resources to support that expected transition activity. In so doing, you help avoid throwing yourself off balance.

Have a Personal Plan

A personal plan will naturally become apparent as you follow the sequence of events suggested in this chapter. Begin your personal plan by determining your personal values to create a purpose statement, clarifying personal passions, and establishing values-based personal money and time management. The very process of assessing whether your use of money and time reflects your values will invariably draw attention to areas exerting an influence that conflicts with your values. As each of these conflicts becomes clear, select an action step to enable you to change course appropriately to bring that influence into alignment with your stated values.

Commit to each action step in writing, and determine a time frame in which to accomplish it. It is also helpful to have a source of support such as a spouse, partner, friend, or mentor. Use your support source to help and encourage you to achieve this goal—and to keep you accountable. What evolves from this strategy is a Personal Plan that will look like the one illustrated in Table 9.7.

Display this action plan in a prominent place in your home where you will see it daily. You might attach it to a bathroom mirror, bedroom mirror, or kitchen refrigerator. Once a year, make it a habit to review your personal plan. Update it as appropriate and as components of the plan are completed successfully. This posted plan will serve to remind you of your most important personal tasks and of the personal priorities for your time, your money, and your other limited resources.

Balance Your Life

As discussed previously in Chapter 1, and in greater detail with strategies in Chapter 6, balancing your life is perhaps the most important step you can take to insulate yourself from the ravages of medical practice stress

Table 9-7: Sample Personal Plan

Your Personal Plan			
Category of Action	**Action Step**	**Start Date**	**Support Source**
Personal Purpose			
Personal Passions			
Purpose Statement			
Life Balance			
Time Management			
Financial Management			
Other			

difficult to accomplish peacefully without a professional facilitator. Just as in a good marriage, physician partners should not permit rancor, disagreements, or differences in perspective to erode their relationships. Effective medical groups recognize and appreciate the value of diversity among partners. Peaceful resolutions to all group conflicts, acceptable to all parties, should be the goal. Without this objective, resentments and bitterness often erode the partnership good will. Unattended to, such resentments inevitably resurface to cause problems.

A potential new physician partner would be well advised to investigate a group's practice perspective and priorities by asking the partners to discuss the values and goals of the partnership and vice versa. The responses should be weighed against the potential new partner's own personal and professional values and priorities to verify that there is a good match. Similarly, the medical group members should satisfy themselves that any potential new partner is reasonably well aligned with the group's practice style and priorities. Any potential or existing conflicts should be explored and negotiated openly before a commitment to each other is made by either party.

The regular exchange of values and expectations for the practice is a key element to the smooth functioning and continued growth of the partnership. There must be fundamental agreement about the clinical service commitments of the partners, the manner of physician practice coverage, leadership and the delegation of responsibility, and the specifics of managing the practice. This will be discussed in greater detail in the following section.

Although not all physicians are equally blessed with the personality and interpersonal skills to be effective group managers, those who assume the role should receive recognition and adequate compensation for the added stress resulting from—along with the time they invest and the commitment they make to—medical group leadership and management. This compensation best takes the form of time away from patient care or additional income, or both. Without one or both of these rewards, there is a disincentive to take on the responsibility of group leadership. Additional financial incentive systems are also effective in rewarding managing physicians who expand group income through mergers, acquisitions, new contracting, or entrepreneurial ventures.

Develop a Practice Plan

The second task that effective medical partners must face is the creation of a practice plan. The practice plan is a working document that provides a road map for the partners to follow as they work to grow the business. It provides specific guidelines for managing the day-to-day affairs of the practice; in addition, it also establishes a long-range strategy for growing and developing the practice.

The practice plan first and foremost commits to expressing the vision, values, and goals of the partners. If differences in goals, priorities, or values exist between partners, the plan should address those differences so there are no hidden agendas and so that the partners' mutual expectations are clear.

The practice plan must also address the clinical objectives and priorities of the practice partners. This includes the "where" and the "how" of the practice; its location, the hours of service, the types of services to be provided, and the clinical coverage and cross-coverage policies. The basic structure of the outpatient practice should be defined, including the anticipated number and types of employees. It addresses the manner by which and by whom the practice will be administered and managed; and defines both administrative and management lines of authority. It also outlines the system for medical billing and the income arrangements of the physician partners flowing from their patient care services. The ancillary professional services needed by the partnership are defined, including legal services, accounting services, insurance services, and retirement plan services. The details of the practice administrative and management plan should lead to the creation of legal documents spelling out the understanding between physician partners. This takes the form of partnership agreements, employment agreements, and shareholder agreements, including partner buy and sell agreements. These documents typically are drawn up by a medical practice consultant.

The plan outlines both the short- and long-term goals of the partners and a five-year business plan to achieve those goals, including the tools and parameters that will be used to assess progress. Potential obstacles to the success of the plan, strategies to overcome those obstacles, and professional competition to the partnership should be assessed. To facilitate the drafting of this practice plan, the partners may seek the input of a business development professional who specializes in medical practices. Such a person may be used in a consultative capacity or may become an employee of the medical corporation on a permanent basis.

Because the current practice environment is characterized by turbulence and continuous change, the practice plan will need to be revisited at least yearly to determine whether revisions are necessary to reflect the changing marketplace and the evolving skills and values of the partners.

Develop an Employee Manual

Just as the practice plan is a road map for the physician partners in the effective medical practice, so is a properly executed employee manual a road map for the nonphysician employees of the practice. It provides the boundaries within which the work environment is defined and defines all work-related policies and procedures. Each employee should read and sign a copy of the manual when hired.

The employee manual should begin with a written history of the practice and of the practice partners. It should specify the values and vision of the physician partners and should clarify the organizational structure of the medical group. In addition, it should clarify physicians' expectations regarding the treatment of patients and referring physicians by employees of the practice.

A section on employment policy should outline employees' rights and protections, management's rights and expectations, working hours, hours of operation, break and meal policies, and vacation and sick leave policies. It should discuss employee records, resignations, dismissal policy, promotion policy, and performance and salary review procedures. Policies regarding requirements for continuing education, licensing, and recertification should be specified for licensed professional employees.

Disciplinary and grievance policies should be delineated, as well as dress codes and behavioral expectations. The latter should address attitude and conduct in the workplace, and should stress the importance of confidentiality of medical information. It should clarify that the rules regarding appropriate dress, behavior, and attitudes are applicable to physicians and nonphysician workers alike.

A separate section should address benefit programs, including eligibility for and vesting of all insurance, health, and retirement benefits. Policy regarding absences from work, tardiness, vacation and holiday leave, medical leave, and sickness should be defined.

The employee manual is a vital document. It serves to prevent confusion; and it protects the practice from unreasonable demands, unrealistic expectations, and inappropriate behavior. It also diminishes the risk of litigation over unfair labor practice. The more specific the manual's language, the smaller is the risk that an employee will unfairly manipulate the system to his or her advantage. Before putting the manual into effect, make sure to have it reviewed by the corporate attorney representing your practice.

Acquire Other Professional Services

The effective medical practice group will require the support of a number of other nonphysician professionals for business support and development. These include insurance professionals, legal professionals, accounting professionals, and financial services professionals.

Insurance is a vital source of protection for the medical professional. Contemporary practices take advantage of many forms of liability protection, which always include some or all of the following: medical malpractice insurance, business insurance for the outpatient office, health insurance for self and dependents; and accident, disability, long-term care, umbrella liability, homeowners, and automobile liability insurance coverage. The scope and variety of these plans often demand the oversight and expertise of more than one insurance professional. Insurance brokers offer the advantage of being able to offer insurance packages from multiple vendors, and in so doing can provide a spectrum of coverage at prices to fit different budgets.

Obtaining corporate legal services to represent the interests of the medical group is a must in the current health care environment. Look for legal specialists who focus on health care law. Such law firms often represent multiple medical group practices and are best able to offer informed opinions on the variety of matters that are relevant to contemporary medical practice. Their expertise must include—but not be limited to—third-party payer contracting, medical mergers and acquisitions, employment issues relevant to medical groups, and payment and reimbursement concerns. All of these issues are in constant turmoil within an industry milieu that is characterized by continuous change and increasing hostility among physician groups, hospital organizations, and third party payers.

The effective medical group practice will also require accounting services that are fully integrated with the group's billing and record-keeping programs and, when possible and appropriate, that also interface with the billing software of the local hospital network(s). The accounting firm should offer automated monthly reporting to the medical practice that tracks gross charges, net receipts, net charges, accounts receivable, and adjustments and bad debt. It should also provide the capability of assessing accounts by age.

The accounting firm must be familiar with the economic and reimbursement issues of the medical practice and it should assist in the monitoring of financial performance on at least a quarterly basis. It will also prepare all state and federal tax returns both for the corporation and, typically, for the medical partners as well. To monitor practice financial performance and to best make use of the group's accounting professionals, the medical group should create a finance committee composed of the appropriate executive officers plus any other interested physicians who are willing and able to track the financial performance of the group on a monthly basis.

Finally, the medical group will require the support of an aggressive and flexible financial services team to handle banking, payroll, and borrowing needs. Comparison shopping within your own community will always reveal the best comprehensive banking program for the practice.

The successful banking organization should provide a package of services, including competitive rates for both corporate and individual loans, corporate and individual banking, corporate and individual lines of credit, credit cards, and highly individualized personal financial services for physician partners and their families.

Reassess Your Practice Frequently

Can an effective medical practice group longer sit back on its heels and thrive simply by providing good medical care to patients? The answer is no. The dynamic world of health care economics and politics demands that physicians maintain a vigil on their business at all times.

This means establishing oversight and practice maintenance systems that monitor physician performance, patient care quality and satisfaction, and the efficiency of support services and medical billing. Individual physician partners or physician committees should be responsible for these oversight responsibilities and report to the partners on a monthly basis.

At least once annually, the physician partners should meet in a retreat setting to review the clinical and business performance of the practice. Reports from the various professional practice consultants utilized by the group should be a routine part of this analysis. The partners should reassess the business plan for the practice and their own professional and personal goals. An objective evaluation whether each physician's performance, personal goals, and professional objectives remain aligned with those of the group should be performed. When necessary, changes in individual physicians' work patterns or attitudes should be addressed through the open exchange of feedback.

You can anticipate that over the course of time, professional transitions will occur among physician partners. They should be anticipated and addressed whenever possible, with respect for the need for change and the value of diversity within the medical group. Transitions to part-time practice are becoming increasingly common and require thoughtful, creative solutions to be effective both for the medical group and for the individual physicians. Such transitions can work well as long as the financial impact of part-time practice, from the standpoint of income and benefits, is revenue-neutral to other full-time physicians. Maintaining revenue neutrality can be accomplished by making benefits proportional to percent of clinical effort, and by encouraging job-sharing when more than one partner desires part-time status.

In Summary

The process of creating a new professional medical practice requires both personal tasks and professional tasks. Both kinds of tasks require of physicians hard work, discipline, courage, and self-awareness. The end result of these two parallel processes must be physicians and organizations that are effective, resilient, and responsive to the winds of constant change.

The personal tasks demand a reassessment of each physician's values, sense of purpose, personal passions, and use of time and money. Frequently physicians have not given conscious thought to these issues since college, or even longer. A synthesis of these important parts of character results in a new awareness of what is important today. They permit the physician to develop an individualized plan yielding personal effectiveness and life balance. Ultimately this permits physicians to link their inner selves with their outer work.

The professional tasks require first and foremost communication and coordination of the newly developed personal plans of all potential physician partners. Similar communication must address the professional goals of all partners. From this sharing will emerge a practice plan that meets the personal and professional needs of all partners while assuring an effective organizational and leadership structure, and a five-year business plan. The organization will be strengthened by the creation of an employee manual that fully explores the rules, boundaries, rights, and responsibilities of each employee. The new practice must also secure professional services for insurance, accounting, legal, and financial services support.

Once so established, regular meetings of the physician staff should occur for the purpose of reassessing their vision and goals; the performance of physician partners; the practice plan; quality of care and patient satisfaction; and medical billing. At least once a year the partners should meet to discuss whether to create new and/or modify the existing business plan. The dynamic and consistent participation of all physician partners at these meetings can be expected to sustain the momentum and spirit of the practice.

References

1. Hudson FM. *The Adult Years: Mastering the Art of Self-Renewal.* San Francisco, Calif: Jossey Bass; 1990, revised 1999.

2. Hudson F, McLean P. *LifeLaunch, A Passionate Guide to the Rest of Your Life.* Santa Barbara, Calif: The Hudson Press; 1995, revised 2000.

Glossary

Asset Allocation: The process of determining what proportions of your portfolio holdings are to be invested in the various *asset classes.*

Asset Class: A standard term that broadly defines a category of potential investments. Examples include large Company Domestic Stock, Small Company Domestic Stock, International Equity, Domestic Fixed Income, and International Fixed Income.

Asset Mix: The percentage weightings (or mix) of different asset classes to be held in the portfolio. There may be separate asset mixes for the taxable and tax-deferred holdings in a portfolio. The composite asset mix represents the total combination of taxable and tax-deferred holdings.

Cash Equivalents: Instruments of high liquidity and safety with a known market value and a very short-term maturity. Examples include treasury bills and money market funds.

Compound Interest: Interest that is computed on the principal and on the interest accrued during the preceding period. Interest may be computed daily, monthly, quarterly, semiannually, or annually for compounding purposes.

Corporate Bonds: Debt instruments issued by private corporations.

Cost Basis: Generally the original purchase price, including loads and other broker commissions, for an asset. Capital gain is calculated by subtracting the cost basis from the sale price of a security.

Defined Benefit Plan: A qualified retirement plan under which a retiring employee will receive a specified amount of money, either in a lump sum or in installments.

Defined Contribution Plan: A qualified retirement plan under which the annual contribution is made by the employer for the benefit of the employee. The employee's retirement benefit will be subject to the amount in the plan at the time of their retirement.

Efficient Frontier: Plots the asset mixes, ranging from conservative to aggressive, that provide the best trade-off of risk and return. "Efficient" asset mixes provide (1) the maximum available assumed return for a given level of risk and (2) the minimum available level of risk for a given level of assumed return.

Inflation: Condition in which the overall prices of goods and services continue to rise, usually caused by an undue expansion in paper money and credit relative to the supply of goods. In the United States the rate of inflation is measured by the consumer price index.

International Equities: Equity securities investment in developed countries throughout the world, excluding the United States.

Large Domestic Stocks: Equity securities of large capitalization companies in the United States.

Long Term Government Bonds: Securities issued by the United States government and debt issues of federal agencies having a maturity of ten years or more.

Municipal Bonds: Debt obligation of a state or local government entity. Exempt from the federal income taxes.

Qualified Retirement Plan: A pension or profit sharing plan established by an employer for the benefit of employees in conformity with specific IRS rules.

Real Estate: Raw land and physical improvements related to it. May be held as a direct investment, or as a limited or general partnership.

Risk: The unpredictability of investment returns. The chance that the actual return from investment in an asset class will be different from its assumed return. Risk is measured statistically using *standard deviation.*

Rollover: Reinvestment of a lump sum distribution from a qualified retirement plan into an individual retirement account, while maintaining tax deferred status.

Small Domestic Stocks: Equity securities of small capitalization companies in the United States.

Standard Deviation: A statistical measurement of dispersion about a mean, which, for a portfolio, depicts how widely the returns varied over a certain period of time. Investors use the standard deviation of historical performance to try to predict the range of returns that are most likely for a given portfolio. When a portfolio a high standard deviation, the predicted range of performance is wide, implying greater volatility.

Term Life Insurance: A life insurance policy written to cover a specified period of time only.

Total Return: The combined return in current income and capital appreciation from investment in an *asset class.*

Umbrella Liability Insurance: Insurance coverage in excess of underlying liability policies, which may also provide coverage for situations excluded by underlying policies.

Universal Life Insurance: A life insurance policy that accumulates cash values. The policy provides flexibility of premium payments.

Variable Life Insurance: A life insurance policy in which the cash values are invested in investment sub-accounts, which include various stock and bond instruments.

Whole Life Insurance: A life insurance policy that remains in force for the insured's lifetime, unless the policy lapses. Whole life insurance policies accumulate a cash value, and provide for fixed premiums.

Internet Resources

Excellent resource for financial calculators, seminar information, and timely articles for physicians: www.mediqus.com

One of the most comprehensive glossaries of financial terms anywhere: www.investorwords.com

Excellent news summaries and financial links: www.investorguide.com

Great site for charting individual securities and technical analysis: www.bigcharts.com

Objective reviews of mutual funds and stocks: www.morningstar.com

Bloomberg online: www.bloomberg.com

Barron's online: www.barrons.com

Smartmoney online: www.smartmoney.com

CNBC online: www.cnbc.com

Index

M

Career *Planning* Guides
for Physicians

Evaluating and Negotiating Your Compensation Arrangements

Learn to negotiate with confidence! This concise book brings you up to speed quickly on how to negotiate the most rewarding and equitable compensation package possible.

Order #: OP206597BJX
Price: $39.95   AMA Member Price: $29.95

The Physician's Resume and Cover Letter Workbook

This easy-to-use workbook makes outlining, composing, and sending a professional resume or CV easier and less intimidating. Includes sample cover letters and resumes that target a full range of medical careers.

Order #: OP206497BJX
Price: $33.00   AMA Member Price: $25.00

Phone orders: 800 621-8335
Secured online orders: www.ama-assn.org/catalog

VISA, MasterCard, American Express and Optima accepted. State sales tax and shipping/ handling charges apply. Satisfaction guaranteed or return within 30 days for full refund.

Get 3rd Book FREE!

Buy *Evaluating & Negotiating Your Compensation Arrangements* and *The Physician's Resume & Cover Letter Workbook* at regular price, and get *The Physician in Transition: Managing the Job Interview* **FREE!**

Order #: OP089001BJX
Price: $72.95   AMA Member Price: $54.95

American Medical Association
Physicians dedicated to the health of America

A Guide for Keeping Physicians Healthy

This practical guide for physicians and their families helps foster a better understanding of the health care needs of physicians, the barriers to their getting appropriate care, and the ways to improve the care itself. Covering scientific, clinical, regulatory, and policy issues germane to many physician health-related topics, this book provides the most current research and thinking in a readable, reference format.

The Handbook of Physician Health reviews the known risk factors for physicians, and discusses approaches or programs that have proven effective. From the stress of residency to the effects of aging, this book covers health issues faced in every stage of the physician life-cycle.

The Essential Guide to understanding the Health Care Needs of Physicians

Phone orders: 800 621-8335
Secured online orders:
www.ama-assn.org/catalog

The Handbook of Physician Health
Order#: OP720399BHS
Price: $42.95
AMA Member Price: $32.95

VISA, MasterCard, American Express and Optima accepted. State sales tax and shipping/handling charges apply. Satisfaction guaranteed or return within 30 days for full refund.

AMA press

American Medical Association
Physicians dedicated to the health of America